CURVY GIRL
crochet

25 Patterns
that Fit and Flatter

Mary Beth Temple

The Taunton Press

 **The Taunton Press**
Inspiration for hands-on living®

The Taunton Press, Inc.
63 South Main Street
PO Box 5506
Newtown, CT 06470-5506
e-mail: tp@taunton.com

Editors: Shawna Mullen and Renee I. Neiger
Developmental editor: Rebecca Behan
Test crocheters: Cathleen Dipierro, Andrea Giattini, Tracy Rivers, Deb Seda, and Nancy Smith
Copy editor: Betty Christiansen
Indexer: Jay Kreider
Cover and interior design: Carol Singer
Layout: Sandra Mahlstedt
Illustrators: Christine Erikson and Charles Voth
Photographer: Susan Pittard
Stylist: Tiffany Pasqualone Ramos
Hair and makeup: Agata Helena

The following names/manufacturers appearing in *Curvy Girl Crochet* are trademarks: Berroco® Vintage™,
Caron®, Lion Brand® Yarn Amazing®, Lion Brand® Yarn Wool-Ease®, Patons®, Plymouth Yarn® Company Zino,
Premier™ Yarns, Red Heart® Luster Sheen®, Red Heart® Super Saver®, Rowan® Panama, SOYSILK®.

Hook Sizing and Abbreviations information (p. 144) and Standard Yarn Weights (p. 146) courtesy of the
Craft Yarn Council, www.yarnstandards.com.

LIBRARY OF CONGRESS CATALOGING-IN-PUBLICATION DATA
Temple, Mary Beth.
  Curvy girl crochet : 25 patterns that fit and flatter / Mary Beth Temple.
    pages cm
  Summary: "This book contains clean, classic patterns including jackets, cardigans, pullovers, sweaters, shawls, shrugs, and more
designed for the plus-size figure, with techniques and schematics to show crocheters exactly how to trouble shoot to solve their
pattern-fitting problems"-- Provided by publisher.
  ISBN 978-1-60085-412-5 (pbk.)
  1. Crocheting--Patterns. 2. Plus-size women's clothing. I. Title.
  TT825.T42 2012
  746.434--dc23
                    2012014195

PRINTED IN THE UNITED STATES OF AMERICA
10 9 8 7 6 5 4 3 2 1

Acknowledgments

So many people to thank, so little space!

First, I want to thank guest designers Marly Bird, Andee Graves, Lindsey Stephens, Charles Voth, and Karen Ratto Whooley for their stylish contributions to this book. My heartfelt gratitude goes to Cathleen Dipierro, Andrea Giattini, Tracy Rivers, Deb Seda, and Nancy Smith—the fearless crochet crew who created many of the beautiful samples and who deciphered my early chicken-scratch patterns. For technical support, many thanks go to Andrea Giattini, Ashley Little, and Charles Voth. All errors are mine; all saves are theirs.

I also gratefully acknowledge the yarn and notion companies who generously donated materials used to make the samples photographed for this book.

Thanks to the whole Taunton Press crew, especially to my original editor Erica Sanders-Foege, to my new editor Shawna Mullen, and to photo editor Katy Binder.

And finally, special thanks to my agent, Kate Epstein, who is perhaps the most reliable person on the planet. If my head hasn't exploded yet, she gets the credit!

25 Patterns
that Fit and Flatter

Contents

Introduction

One thing I've learned from years of designing patterns: If you put 50 plus-sized women in a room, no two of them will be plus-sized in quite the same way.

I worried about this when I began creating this book—how would I come up with patterns that would suit everyone? In the end, I decided that this was a wonderful opportunity to create flattering garments for all sorts of different body types. Not every piece will suit every body, but everybody will find something within these pages that will satisfy their need to create and to express their individual styles. After all, aren't cookie-cutter clothes what we are trying to step away from?

You know what will suit everybody? Crochet! While you may have heard that crochet garments weren't flattering for plus-sized figures, those bulky, boxy garment shapes referred to by the crochet naysayers are a thing of the past. Contemporary crochet designers know what you are about to find out—that using lightweight yarns, open stitch patterns, garment shaping, or a combination of all three creates beautiful garments with style and drape. Crochet really does lend itself to garments that fit and flatter.

In this book you'll find crocheted pullovers, cardigans, coats, wraps, jackets, and more. An entire wardrobe of year-round looks, designed with your curves in mind. But I've also included tips, tricks, and techniques for determining how to alter these patterns to fit your unique shape. I know most of you will skip over the instructional material at the beginning of this book and turn right to the eye candy—the patterns! But I do hope you read over all of that mathy goodness in chapters 1 and 2 before you start stitching. In the back of the book you'll find stitch patterns, yarn information, and a host of other resources, although I can't say I blame you for heading right for the good stuff.

So turn the pages and explore the possibilities. Your style, your body, your turn!

—*Mary Beth Temple*

CHAPTER
1

Projects that Fit and Flatter

ONE OF THE FATAL FLAWS WE ALL ENCOUNTER WHEN CREATING or shopping for plus-size clothing is that three different women who normally wear, for example, a size 3X could be built three different ways. Our clothing has to be chosen not just based on our measurements but also on our shapes.

So let's take the time right now to think in broad strokes about what we want in a crochet garment. In this chapter, we will analyze our unique body characteristics. Then we will analyze garment details to open our minds to styles and shapes we may not have considered before.

We will get more specific later, but for now, commit to see past what you might normally crochet. The perfect garment for you might just be something you've never tried before.

Try on all kinds of things, not just your old standby shapes and colors—or size! In fact, make a point of trying on some garments that are a size or two up or down from what you normally select. Let go of what you think that size label should say. The size that flatters you most may change from manufacturer to manufacturer, and even from garment shape to garment shape. Take a trusted friend or family member if you can—another set of eyes might make selections you wouldn't have dreamed of, and if nothing else, having great company will make the afternoon a fun adventure, rather than dreaded homework.

You might be surprised to find something that looks marvelous on you that you skipped before out of habit—and you will definitely find some shapes that you know you will never want to wear. Remember, there is no right or wrong in the trying-on stage. The hours spent trying on sweaters that someone else made will save you days of wasted effort, to say nothing of cold hard cash, trying to get good results from a pattern that just won't suit you, no matter what.

Make detailed notes of the shapes and colors that flatter you most, paying special attention to details like sleeve types (raglan, set-in, drop, and so on), necklines

Finding shapes that flatter

What shape are you? Take a look in the mirror. Remember, we are looking at shape and proportion here, not actual measurements. No matter what your shape, fit is the most important thing to consider. Your garment should neither be baggy enough to serve as an emergency sleeping bag, nor tight enough that there is a pool going on in the office as to when that button will pop.

All of the fabric should skim the body, more closely in the areas you wish to draw attention to, less closely in the areas you wish to visually ignore. This means that the garment pieces need to be shaped. I don't care how great a stitcher you are, you are not going to get a flattering sweater out of a bunch of rectangles.

Choose a pattern detail with the same theory in mind; a color contrast, embellishment, or tricky stitch pattern is going to draw the eye. Place it where you want that wandering eye to rest, not directly on the body part you consider to be your problem area.

Perhaps the best way for you to decide what will look best on your unique body is to try on as many shapes and styles of clothing as you have access to in order to see what makes you feel and look your best. Start with your well-loved favorites from the closet, but then make a day of it and hit all the local ready-to-wear stores that stock your size.

Measure Before You Begin

WHAT TO MEASURE	MEASUREMENT IN INCHES
Bust	
Waist	
High Hip	
Low Hip	
Bicep	
Center Back Neck to Waist	
Shoulder to Shoulder Back	
Arm Length from Shoulder	
Inside Arm Length from Underarm	

(square, scoop, round, and V-neck), and garment length (waist, hip, or thigh length).

Measuring for fit

Now that you have information on what type of project looks good on you, it's time to think crochet. And the first thing you need is accurate information on the person you are crocheting for—yourself!

Grab that friend you took shopping and plan an afternoon to measure each other. While you can absolutely measure yourself, the buddy system provides more accurate results.

It's hard to believe that just nine numbers could have such a big impact, but as you'll see as you work your way through the patterns in this book, accurate measurements are essential for a good fit. Fill out the "Measure Before You Begin" chart with all your information.

Choosing the best yarn

You know which garment you want to make, you know how you want it to fit. Now let's talk about what you want to make it from—the yarn.

Here are some aspects to consider.

YARN WEIGHT

Bulky yarn gives you bulky finished items, which are not particularly flattering in larger sizes, except, on occasion, as outerwear. Shop the corner of the yarn store where you find lighter-weight yarns—lace, fingering, DK, and light worsteds.

FIBER CONTENT

There are so many combinations of both natural and man-made fibers available on the market right now that it would be impossible to lay down a hard-and-fast rule on what fiber content is the best choice for your specific project. But the most important characteristics to consider when choosing a yarn—drape, warmth, and ease of care and cleaning—are linked to the type of fiber it is made from.

Drape. Bamboo and silk yarns hang differently when crocheted than wools and acrylics do, so make sure to tailor the fiber content you choose to the type of fabric you are looking for in the finished item.

Warmth. Some fibers run warmer than others. Lofty animal fibers such as alpaca and angora are particularly high on the toasty list. Certain 100 percent acrylic yarns also trap heat because they don't breathe, even though they are light in weight. If you tend to feel warm indoors, save these yarns for outerwear or cold climate living.

Care and cleaning. Be honest with yourself: Are you likely to hand wash and dry your sweater flat every time you wear it? Or are you much more likely to throw it in the washer and dryer, and devil take the hindmost? Do you have kids or pets or a job that makes your garment more likely to get soiled in one way or another? After all of the effort of crocheting your own garment, make sure you will be able to care for it so it lasts a long time.

Yarn Tips

Yarn is more than the sum of its fiber content or its dye job. How the yarn is made affects the look of a finished garment, as well as how hard wearing it is.

TWIST
Smooth yarn with a good amount of twist offers crisp stitch definition for patterns that feature textured stitch detailing, such as the Sweetheart Tank Top (p. 50), or cables, such as the Intertwined Poncho (p. 86).

PLIES
Single-ply yarn, while often beautiful, is fragile and tends to pill. Avoid single-ply yarns for garments you will wear often, and when using more than one yarn in a project, keep single-ply yarns away from high-stress areas like elbows and button bands.

HALO
Halo refers to a yarn's fuzz factor. Mohair and angora are yarns with lots of halo, great for simple or openwork stitching, but not so hot for dense or textured stitching because the halo obscures the work.

ELASTICITY
Wools and wool blends are springy—they stretch and relax with your natural movement. Cottons, silks, and linens, however, have no elasticity and may sag or stretch out in time. Match yarn and pattern accordingly.

COST

Everyone is on a budget, and it makes good sense to project your garment's cost not only in materials but also in upkeep. That said, the least expensive skein is not always the best choice. Choose materials that will look good and last a long time to give you the biggest payoff for the effort necessary to create a well-fitted garment. This is an investment in your wardrobe that will last for years to come.

Also consider the yardage in a skein. The per-skein price matters a lot less than the total project cost; the more yardage on the skein, the lower the number of skeins needed to complete your project.

COLOR

All of the colors of the rainbow are out there, but you don't have to use all of them in one project, even though many of them seem to find their way into your shopping basket at the yarn store. Take into account your personal preference, but also think about how you will wear your garment and what you will wear it with. Not everything has to be neutral, but make sure you plan ahead to get the most use possible from this wardrobe investment. Some pieces can be workhorses and some can be show ponies; just try to avoid making all of one or the other.

Another way to consider color in your piece is to finesse the placement of light and dark colors. Dark colors recede; light colors draw the eye. So in a sweater with more than one color in it, you can place the darker colors on the areas you don't wish to draw attention to, and the lighter colors on your favorite features. In the Progressive Tunic (p. 35), for example, I used the darker colors on the hem and the lighter colors at the neck to draw attention away from my stomach and toward my face. But if you are more top heavy, you might want to start with the light colors at the bottom and graduate to the darker colors to draw attention to your waist and away from your bust. Color changes are the easiest modifications to make!

Finding Your Fit

WE HAVE ALREADY ESTABLISHED THAT NO TWO PLUS-SIZED women are shaped exactly the same way, but how does one go about making a fabulous-fitting sweater from a pattern that is close, but not quite perfect?

The word is *modification*—meaning you are not going to follow the pattern blindly as written, but will take a look at each individual part of the garment and change (modify) what you need to suit your particular shape.

The most important piece of information in the whole process is your gauge. Not my gauge, not the gauge of your friend who made the same sweater, not what you think your gauge might be—*your* actual gauge. The gauge that you got using the yarn you are going to use in the project and the hook that you are going to use in the project, treated in the same way you will treat the finished garment.

Using gauge swatches

Okay, a lot of you want to stop reading now because you hate to do gauge swatches. You have ignored people who have told you to do them in the past and you swear you aren't going to start now.

But here's the deal—if you want your sweater to fit and flatter and you are going to go through the effort of planning your project modifications, the starting data has to be real or it's a waste of time. Here are five tips to get an accurate gauge measurement:

YARN

Use the yarn destined for use in your project. While many yarn companies mark their yarns with the CYCA (Craft Yarn Council of America) number designating its weight, there can be wide variations within each weight category. Many of us substitute yarn we prefer for the yarn used in a pattern. When checking out suitable yarn substitutes, make use of the fact that the CYCA number is listed for each pattern in this book, but remember that not all yarns with the same CYCA numbers are perfectly interchangeable. If you are concerned about wasting cash on yarn you might not use, purchase a single skein of the yarn you are considering, crochet your gauge swatch, and then go back to purchase the rest of your yarn if you are happy with the results. If the yarn doesn't quite work out, you will only be out the cost of the single skein. That's a lot more time- (and cost-) effective than wasting a lot of effort and cash on a yarn that fights you the whole way.

HOOKS

Use the hook you will use in your project. It's hard to believe, but the same stitcher using the same yarn will more than likely get different gauges when using different hooks—especially in the row gauge. Aluminum, wood, plastic—whatever your hook preference is, stitch your gauge swatch with that type of hook. Also, check the millimeter size marked on your hook; not every hook manufacturer uses the same millimeter for a marked U.S. size. If you are in the habit of looking for a G hook rather than a 4-mm hook, you may be surprised in the difference between brands.

SIZE

Don't skimp on size. Your swatch should be a minimum of 4 in. square, but bigger is better.

BLOCKING

Block the swatch before you measure. If you are going to hand wash the garment, hand wash the swatch. If you are going to toss the finished item in the washer and dryer, do that to the swatch as well. Few things are more frustrating than creating the perfect garment only to have it change shape after it's washed. If you worry that inelastic fibers such as cotton or bamboo may stretch out of shape when crocheted, pin your swatch to a bulletin board and let gravity do its work for a couple of days. If the yarn stretches out in swatch form, your finished garment will stretch out, too—but even more so, as a garment is heavier than a swatch.

STITCH COUNT

Take your stitch-count measurements from the center of the swatch. Stitches near the beginning, the end, or either side will be pulled slightly out of shape. The center stitches are the most accurate representation of the bulk of the stitching in your garment.

Troubleshooting

Now that you have your gauge swatch, take a good look at it. Is it the same as the gauge listed in the pattern, and are you pleased with the look of the fabric? If yes, then this is excellent news. Move on to the next step, assessing the pattern.

If the answer is no, first examine the look of the fabric. If you are happy with it, you might want to leave well enough alone and stitch with the hook you used for the swatch, making some adjustments in the pattern size you select. If not, make another swatch using a different size hook. Go up a hook size if your fabric looks too dense and tight. Go down a hook size if it looks too loose or floppy. Repeat the process until you have a swatch that makes you happy—that is, one that looks good and is the same as or pretty darn close to the gauge noted in the pattern you wish to make.

Assessing the pattern

You have accurate measurements of your body and accurate measurements of your gauge, so now what?

Take a look at the schematics of the garment you want to crochet. Make a copy of the pattern and schematics so you can take notes on the changes you wish to make. Writing down changes means you can stitch with confidence, and if you take a little project break, you won't come back wondering what the heck you were doing.

The schematics reflect the finished size of the individual pattern pieces for every size in which the pattern is offered. To make life easier, go ahead and circle the measurements that correspond to the size you are making.

Determining ease

Compare your measurements to the measurements on the schematic for the size you would like to make. Are they an exact match? Probably not!

Modify for Ease

GARMENT STYLE	ADD TO PATTERN (from actual body measurements*)
Close Fitting	1 to 2 in.
Standard Fitting	2 to 4 in.
Loose Fitting	4 to 6 in.
Oversized	6 in. or more

*(or subtract the same amount, for negative ease)

If you have a 46-in. bust and made a sweater that finished at 46 in. at the bust, it would be skin tight, which is fine if that is the look you are after, but most of us like a little breathing room in our wardrobe. The amount of difference between your actual measurement and the finished measurement is called *ease*.

Adapting hemlines and sleeves

Body measurement plus desired ease equals the required finished measurement. Of course, that's *around* our bodies. We also have to be aware of garment length. A 5-ft. 2-in. woman who wears a size 4X is going to need a different length garment than a 5-ft. 10-in. woman who wears a size 4X.

If you made your garment pieces the lengths that are noted in the schematic, where would the garment hem fall on your body? As a general rule, garment hems should not land directly on your widest spot. You might prefer to shorten a garment that falls there so the hemline floats above that line, or lengthen it so it skims the wide spot and falls below it.

Also keep in mind ease of wear. For example, I prefer not to sit on my sweaters, especially if they are made of a yarn like cotton or bamboo, because sitting on the back might make it stretch out a bit and lose its shape. But a long, flowing look might be exactly what you are looking for, so choose to lengthen or shorten according to your taste.

What about the sleeves? Take a moment to double-check the schematic measurements against your measurements to see if you want to lengthen or shorten the sleeves.

Shaping the waist

One of the easiest modifications to make to any sweater is to adjust the waist shaping. All of the waist-shaping instructions for the fitted sweaters in this book are set off in their own section of text. Don't want them? Don't do them! Need them higher or lower? Add or remove rows before the start of the waist-shaping instructions.

Modifying for fit: A sample project

Let's use some sample measurements and the schematic from the Essential Cardigan (p. 64) as an example of how to modify a pattern for a better fit.

Our mythical stitcher, Beth, is 5 ft. 2 in. tall, has a 48-in. bust, a 44-in. waist, and longer-than-average arms.

According to the Sizing Chart on p. 143, her bust-line puts her between sizes XL and 2X. Now she'll take a look at the garment's finished bust measurement. She needs this information to determine the ease, which is calculated by finding the difference between the finished bust measurement and the wearer's actual bust measurement. For the Essential Cardigan, the pattern calls for approximately 4 in. of ease. If Beth would prefer more or less ease in her finished garment, she could simply pick the size that's closest to her desired finished measurements. Or, she could use the following techniques to adjust the pattern for a custom fit.

SWITCH HOOK SIZE

Beth could change the hook size up or down to affect the finished gauge of her piece. If she wants to use the smaller-sized pattern and make it larger, she would go up a hook size or two; if she wants to use the larger-sized pattern and make it smaller, she would go down a hook size or two. This method requires another gauge swatch to be accurate. If you want to change hook sizes, you need to make sure that the stitching is not just larger or smaller, but that it results in a fabric that drapes well and is pleasing to the eye.

ADD OR SUBTRACT STITCHES

If changing the hook size doesn't work for Beth, she might need to add or subtract stitches from the directions. In Beth's case, she should probably stitch the smaller size and add stitches, rather than subtract stitches from the larger size, because she is petite in height.

Beth wants to add 2 in. to the bust of the finished garment. Split that number so you can add half to the back and half to the front—1 in. for each. This pattern's gauge is 14 stitches to 4 in., so she'll add a total of 7 stitches (2 in.)—4 stitches to the front and 3 stitches to the back. If the number of stitches to be added was even, Beth would have added an equal number to front and back, but for uneven numbers, the extra stitch defaults to the front.

Always add or subtract the stitches in an area where there is little or no shaping. Beth will add hers right in the middle of the garment; the neck edge will be slightly wider, but that doesn't bother her. If it did, she would have added the stitches on the sides and incorporated the extra stitches into the armhole shaping.

ADAPT HEM AND SLEEVE LENGTH

Now for the length. Beth wants to take off 3 in. from the garment length so the hem doesn't fall at the widest part of her hip. Because this pattern includes waist shaping, she must decide whether to take off the 3 in. before or after that shaping. Beth compares the measurements on the schematic to her body measurements and decides she will take off 1 in. before the shaping (at the hip) and 2 in. after it.

To adjust the pattern *before* waist shaping, she first will look to the row gauge, which is 8 rows to 4 in., or $\frac{1}{2}$ in. per row. Beth wants to remove 1 in., or 2 rows. So when she comes to the Back instructions, "Rep Row 2 for pattern until 8 (8, 8, 10, 10, 10) rows have been completed," she will cross out the number 8 for size 2X and change it to 6 (p. 65).

To adjust the pattern *after* waist shaping, she will measure her project pieces as she works. When she comes to "Work even on these sts (dc in each dc across) until work measures $15\frac{1}{2}$ ($15\frac{1}{2}$, 16, 17, $17\frac{1}{2}$, $17\frac{1}{2}$) in. from beg," she will work even until the work measures 13 in., instead of the 16 in. written in the text and

continued on page 17

marked on the schematic (p. 69). She will make sure to end with a RS row, or whichever row is designated in the instructions so that she can move right to the armhole as written.

Last, the sleeves need to be crocheted 1½ in. longer than designated in the pattern. Beth will follow the directions as written until she gets to the "work even" section in the Shoulder Shaping instructions; in this case, the instructions say, "Work even on these sts until work measures 15½ (15½, 16, 17, 17½, 17½) in. from beg, ending with a RS row" (p. 67). Beth is going to change that 17½ in. to 19 in., still ending with a RS row, and then move on to the sleeve cap shaping.

The most important thing to remember when working modifications is to make the changes on all of the pieces that mirror or touch each other. If you change the back of a sweater, you need to change the front pieces in the same way. If you change the length of one sleeve, you need to change the length of the other. If you alter the armhole at all, you need to alter the sleeve shaping to match.

Of course, if Beth had chosen to make the Simply Stripes Jacket (p. 81), a garment that is worked vertically (side to side), she would have changed the length of the project by changing the number of stitches in the starting chain, and changed the width of the project by adding or subtracting rows.

After you have planned your math, write the results on both the copy of the schematic and the copy of the text so you don't forget exactly what you wanted to do and when. Note that you may have to purchase an extra skein or two of yarn for the size you are working if you added length or stitches.

When a garment is finished and you know you are completely pleased with the results, you might want to write your modifications into the book so they don't get lost!

Now pick your pattern, make your notes, and get to the fun part—the stitching!

How Finishing Affects Fit

When all of your pieces are stitched and you are ready to finish your garment, you might find the results are almost—but not quite—perfect. Here are three quick tips to make minor tweaks.

1. BLOCK IT.

Sometimes you can make a piece grow or shrink a small amount by blocking it to the exact measurements you want, particularly if you have used a yarn with some animal fiber in it.

2. SEAM IT.

When you are seaming your finished garment, you can often tweak the final measurements by joining together the crocheted pieces a few stitches inward from the edge (to make the garment smaller) or keeping your stitching to the very edge (to make it larger).

3. BUTTON IT.

Moving your buttons a half inch one way or the other is a quick way to ensure you have the fit you want. Moving the buttons more than a half inch may make the closures look either too skimpy or too bulky.

CHAPTER
3

Pullovers, Tunics, and Tank Tops

THIS CHAPTER INCLUDES ALL OF THE TOSS-ON-AND-GO GARMENTS—pullovers, tunics, and tanks. There are projects here that are fitted and some that are A-line, so no matter what your shape, you will find something flattering to make.

If you are new to making or modifying crocheted garments, the sleeveless options—the Sweetheart Tank Top (p. 50), Perfect Base Tank Top (p. 54), and Progressive Tunic (p. 35)—are great starter projects because you don't have to fiddle with sleeves or change armhole shaping. These projects also require less finishing, as there are fewer pieces to stitch together at the end.

Of course, the Essential Pullover (p. 20) is also a great place to start your adventures in modification. It is a simple but beautiful combination of A-line shaping and simple double crochet, so the focus is on the fit rather than the stitching.

Many of the garments in this chapter are perfect layering pieces. Wear the tank tops under your favorite jackets, or toss on the Aperture Tunic (p. 46) or Orange Marmalade Shell (p. 58) over your favorite close-fitting tank or T-shirt.

Essential Pullover

Let's start with a basic double crochet pullover. The simpler the stitching on any garment, the easier to modify the fit, so this is a great first sweater to custom fit to your own measurements. If you can double crochet, you can make a sweater that fits! The Essential Pullover features an A-line, flared fit and three-quarter-length sleeves with a lot of ease. One way to customize the fit of this sweater is to decrease or increase the angle of the flare for a sweater that's a little more or less close fitting.

Tip: Several of the garments in this book have A-line shaping, like the Essential Pullover. However, that shaping won't necessarily translate into a babydoll-style sweater. For those of us who are a little wider at the rib cage or waist than the bust, the shaping will accommodate those inches while giving the appearance of straight side seams.

SKILL LEVEL
Easy

FINISHED BUST
L (XL, 2X, 3X, 4X, 5X); 46 (50, 54, 60, 64, 68) in.

YARN
Berroco® Vintage™ DK; 5 (6, 6, 7, 8, 9) skeins Chana Dal, #2192 (100 g/288 yds); 1,440 (1,728, 1,728, 2,016, 2,304, 2,592) yds DK weight yarn (CYCA 3, Light, see p. 146)

NOTIONS
Hook size G/6 U.S. (4 mm) *or size needed to obtain gauge*
Tapestry needle

GAUGE
14 sts and 8 rows = 4 in. in dc

NOTES
Ch-3 counts as 1 dc throughout.
For crab stitch instructions, see Techniques and Stitches, p. 141.

Back

Ch 102 (109, 116, 125, 132, 141).
Row 1 (WS) Dc in 4th ch from hook and in each ch across. Ch 3, turn. 100 (107, 114, 123, 130, 139) dc.
Rows 2–3 Dc in each dc across. Ch 3, turn.
Row 4 Dc2tog, dc in each dc across until 2 sts remain, dc2tog. 98 (105, 112, 121, 128, 137) dc.
Rep Rows 2–4 for pattern until 80 (87, 94, 103, 110, 119) dc remain.
Work even on these sts if needed until work measures 17 (17, 18, 19, 19½, 19½) in. from beg, ch 1, turn after last row.

ARMHOLE SHAPING

Row 1 Sl st in each of 1st 7 (8, 9, 10, 10, 10) dc, ch 3 (counts as 1 dc), dc in each dc across until 6 (7, 8, 9, 9, 9) dc remain. Ch 3, turn. 68 (73, 78, 85, 92, 101) dc.
Row 2 Dc2tog, dc in each dc across to last 2 sts, dc2tog. Ch 3, turn. 66 (71, 78, 83, 90, 99) dc.
Rows 3–5 Rep Row 2. 60 (65, 72, 77, 84, 93) dc.
Row 6 Dc in each dc across. Ch 3, turn.

continued on page 22

Row 7 Rep Row 2. 58 (63, 68, 75, 84, 91) dc.
Rep Rows 6–7 0 (1, 2, 2, 3, 3) time(s). 58 (61, 64, 71, 78, 85) dc.

Sizes L (XL, 2X) only:
Work even until work measures 9 (9½, 10) in. from the start of the armhole shaping, ending with a RS row.

Sizes 3X (4X, 5X) only:
Rep Rows 6–7 2 (3, 5) more times. 67 (72, 75) dc.
Work even until work measures 10½ (11, 11½) in. from the start of the armhole shaping, ending with a RS row.

I chose a tailored crab stitch trim for this pullover to allow the shape of the sweater to take center stage. If you'd prefer a more delicate trim, just follow the Picot Edging instructions given for the Essential Cardigan (p. 64)

Shoulder Shaping

RIGHT SHOULDER

Row 1 Dc in each of 1st 20 (20, 21, 22, 23, 24) sts. Ch 3, turn.
Row 2 Dc in each of 1st 5 (5, 6, 6, 6, 7) dc, hdc in each of next 5 (5, 5, 6, 6, 6) dc, sc in each of next 5 (5, 5, 5, 6, 6) dc, end off, leaving remaining 5 (all sizes) dc unworked.

LEFT SHOULDER

Row 1 Work in the same direction as Row 1 of the 1st shoulder, sk 18 (21, 22, 23, 26, 27) dc, attach yarn in next dc, ch 3, dc in each dc to end. Ch 1, turn.
Row 2 Sl st in each of 1st 5 dc, sc in each of next 5 (5, 5, 5, 6, 6) dc, hdc in each of next 5 (5, 5, 6, 6, 6) dc, dc in each dc to end. End off.

Front

Rep instructions for Back until Row 5 of armhole shaping is completed.

LEFT FRONT

Row 1 24 (26, 29, 32, 35, 38) dc. Ch 3, turn.
Row 2 Dc2tog, dc in each dc across until 2 dc remain, dc2tog. Ch 3, turn. 22 (24, 27, 30, 33, 36) dc.
Row 3 Dc in each dc across. Ch 3, turn.
Rep Rows 2–3 for pattern until 20 (20, 21, 22, 23, 24) sts remain.
Work even on these sts if necessary until work measures 1 row less than Back from the start of armhole shaping, ending with a RS row.

LEFT SHOULDER

Row 1 Dc in each of 1st 5 (5, 6, 6, 6, 7) dc, hdc in each of next 5 (5, 5, 6, 6, 6) dc, sc in each of next 5 (5, 5, 5, 6, 6) dc, end off, leaving remaining 5 (all sizes) dc unworked.

RIGHT FRONT

Row 1 Work in same direction as Row 1 of Left Front, sk 20 (21, 20, 21, 22, 23) dc, attach yarn with sl st in next dc, ch 3, dc in each dc to end. Ch 1, turn. 24 (26, 29, 32, 35, 38) dc.
Rep instructions for Left Front beginning with Row 2.

RIGHT SHOULDER

Row 1 Sl st in each of 1st 5 dc, sc in each of next 5 (5, 5, 5, 6, 6) dc, hdc in each of next 5 (5, 5, 6, 6, 6) dc, dc in each dc to end. End off.

Sleeve (Make 2)

Ch 80 (84, 88, 92, 96, 100).

Row 1 Dc in 4th ch from hook and in each ch across. Ch 3, turn. 78 (82, 86, 90, 94, 98) dc.
Row 2 Work even.
Row 3 Dc2tog, dc in each dc across until 2 dc remain, dc2tog. Ch 3, turn. 76 (80, 84, 88, 92, 96) dc.
Rep Rows 2–3 for pattern until 64 (68, 72, 76, 80, 84) sts remain.
Work even if necessary until sleeve measures 7 (7, 8, 8, 9, 9) in. from beg, ch 1, turn after final row.

SHAPE SLEEVE CAP

Row 1 Sl st in each of 1st 7 (8, 9, 10, 10, 10) dc, ch 3 (counts as 1 dc), dc in each dc across until 6 (7, 8, 9, 9, 9) dc remain. Ch 3, turn. 52 (54, 54, 54, 56, 60) dc.
Row 2 Dc2tog, dc in each dc across to last 2 sts, dc2tog. Ch 3, turn. 50 (52, 52, 52, 54, 58) dc.
Rows 3–5 Rep Row 2. 44 (46, 46, 46, 48, 52) dc.
Row 6 Dc in each dc across. Ch 3, turn.
Row 7 Rep Row 2. 42 (44, 44, 44, 46, 50) dc.
Rep Rows 6–7 0 (1, 2, 2, 3, 3) times. 42 (42, 40, 40, 40, 44) dc. Ch 1, turn after the final Row 7.
Next Row Sl st in each of 1st 4 dc, sc, hdc, dc across until 6 sts remain, hdc, sc, sl st in each of last 4 sts. Ch 1, turn. 42 (42, 40, 40, 40, 44) sts, 30 (30, 28, 28, 28, 32) are dcs.
Next Row Sl st in each of 1st 6 sts, sc, hdc, dc across until 8 sts remain, hdc, sc, sl st, turn. 37 (37, 35, 35, 35, 39) sts, 26 (26, 24, 24, 24, 28) are dcs.
Final Row Sl st in each of 1st 6 sts, sc, hdc, dc in each of next 20 (20, 18, 18, 18, 22) dc, hdc, sc, sl st, end off.

Assembly

Block each garment piece.
Stitch Front to Back at shoulder seams.
Stitch sleeves into armhole openings, easing to fit.
Stitch side seam and sleeve seam on each side.

Edgings

Work 1 rnd sc around hem, each sleeve hem, and neckline.
Work 1 rnd crab st over each sc rnd. End off.

Essential Pullover Schematics

BACK AND FRONT

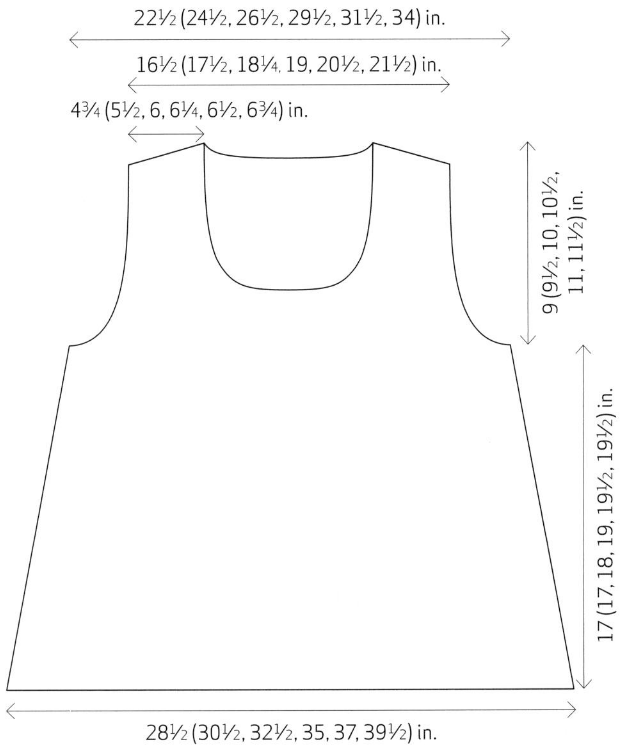
22½ (24½, 26½, 29½, 31½, 34) in.
16½ (17½, 18¼, 19, 20½, 21½) in.
4¾ (5½, 6, 6¼, 6½, 6¾) in.
9 (9½, 10, 10½, 11, 11½) in.
17 (17, 18, 19, 19½, 19½) in.
28½ (30½, 32½, 35, 37, 39½) in.

SLEEVE

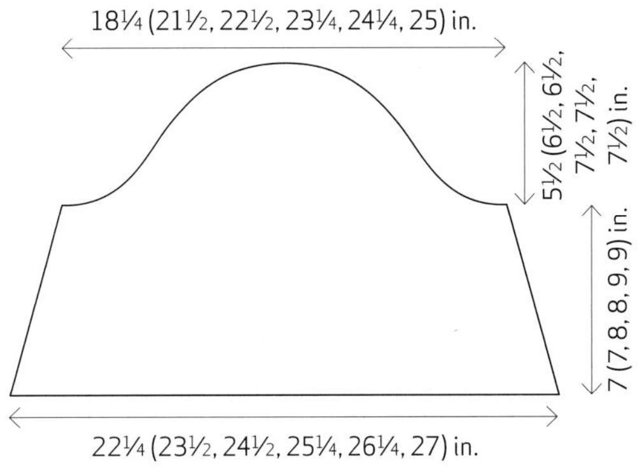
18¼ (21½, 22½, 23¼, 24¼, 25) in.
5½ (6½, 6½, 7½, 7½, 7½) in.
7 (7, 8, 8, 9, 9) in.
22¼ (23½, 24½, 25¼, 26¼, 27) in.

Curvy Cowl-Neck Pullover

Use a soft, silky yarn for this surprisingly quick-to-work-up pullover to get a lovely cowl-neck detail without layers of bulky fabric. The cowl neckline is worked right onto the sweater front, in an easy-to-learn increase of the shell stitch pattern. This is definitely a sweater that looks much harder to make than it actually is!

Tip: Stretchy stitch patterns such as this shell stitch don't cry out for technical waist shaping. The resulting fabric has a lot of give to it, so it will settle where it should on your body without a lot of outside help.

SKILL LEVEL
Intermediate

FINISHED BUST
L (XL, 2X, 3X, 4X, 5X); 46½ (51, 54, 61, 65, 68) in.

YARN
SWTC Pure; 10 (11, 12, 14, 15, 16) skeins Marigold, #028 (50 g/150 m); 1,640 (1,804, 1,968, 2,296, 2,460, 2,624) yds DK weight yarn (CYCA 3, Light, see p. 146)

NOTIONS
Hook size H/8 U.S. (5 mm) *or size needed to obtain gauge*
Tapestry needle

GAUGE
Seven 3-dc shells and 10 rows = 5 in. in patt st

NOTE
Ch-3 counts as 1 dc throughout.

Back

Loosely ch 100 (109, 115, 130, 139, 145).

Row 1 (RS) 3 dc in 5th ch from hook, *sk 2 ch, 3 dc in next ch. Rep from * across until 2 ch remain, sk 1 ch, dc in last ch. Ch 3, turn. 32 (35, 37, 42, 45, 47) 3-dc shells plus 2 dc (ch-3 counts as 1 dc here and throughout).

Row 2 (WS) Sk 1st 2 dc, (dc, ch 1, dc) in next dc (center dc of 3-dc shell), *sk 2 dc, (dc, ch 1, dc) in next dc. Rep from * to end, sk 1 dc, dc in last dc. Ch 3, turn.

Row 3 *3 dc in next ch-1 sp. Rep from * to end, dc in last dc. Ch 3, turn.

Rep Rows 2–3 for pattern until work measures 13½ (13½, 14, 15, 15½, 15½) in. from start, ending with a Row 3. Ch 1, turn after the final Row 3.

ARMHOLE SHAPING

Row 1 Sl st in 1st dc and in each of next 6 (6, 9, 9, 12, 12) dc, ch 3, sk 1 dc (dc, ch 1, dc) in next dc, *sk 2 dc, (dc, ch 1, dc) in next dc. Rep from * until 2 (2, 3, 3, 4, 4) shells remain unworked, sk 1 dc, dc in next dc. Ch 1, turn. 28 (31, 33, 38, 41, 43) shells plus 2 dc.

Row 2 Sl st in 1st dc, sl st in next dc, sl st in ch-1 sp, ch 3, *3 dc in next ch-1 sp. Rep from * until 1 ch-1 sp remains, dc in last ch-1 sp. Ch 3, turn. 26 (29, 31, 36, 39, 41) shells plus 2 dc.

Row 3 Sk 1st 2 dc, (dc, ch 1, dc) in next dc (center dc of 3-dc shell), *sk 2 dc, (dc, ch 1, dc) in next dc. Rep from * to end, sk 1 dc, dc in last dc. Ch 1, turn.

continued on page 26

Rows 4–7 (9, 9, 11, 15, 15) Rep Rows 2–3. Ch 3, turn after the final Row 3. 22 (23, 25, 26, 27, 29) shells plus 2 dc after the last repeat.

Row 8 (10, 10, 12, 16, 16) *3 dc in next ch-1 sp. Rep from * to end, dc in last dc. Ch 3, turn.

Work even by repeating Rows 2–3 of Back if needed, until work measures 10 (10, 11, 11, 12, 12) in. from start of Armhole Shaping, ending with a Row 3.

RIGHT SHOULDER

Row 1 Sk 1st 2 dc, (dc, ch 1, dc) in next dc (center dc of 3-dc shell), *sk 2 dc, (dc, ch 1, dc) in next dc. Rep from * until 5 (5, 6, 6, 6, 7) shells have been completed. Ch 3, turn.

Row 2 3 dc in next ch-1 sp, 3 dc in each of next 1 (1, 1, 1, 1, 2) ch-1 sp(s), 3 hdc in each of next 1 (1, 2, 2, 2, 2) ch-1 sp(s), 3 sc in next ch-1 sp, sl st in next ch-1 sp. End off.

LEFT SHOULDER

Row 1 Working in same direction as Row 1 of Right Shoulder, sk 12 (13, 13, 14, 15, 15) 3-dc shells, (dc, ch 1, dc) in center dc of next 3-dc shell, *sk 2 dc, (dc, ch 1, dc) in next dc. Rep from * to end, sk 1 dc, dc in last dc, ch 1, turn.

Row 2 Sl st in 1st dc, sl st in next dc, sl st in ch-1 sp, 3 sc in next ch-1 sp, 3 hdc in each of next 1 (1, 2, 2, 2, 2) ch-1 sp(s), 3 dc in each of next 2 (2, 2, 2, 2, 3) ch-1 sps. End off.

Front

Rep instructions for Back until Row 7 (7, 7, 9, 9, 11) of Armhole Shaping is complete, ch 3, turn after last row. 22 (25, 27, 30, 33, 33) ch-1 sps plus 2 dc.

Row 8 (8, 8, 10, 10, 12) 2 dc in 1st dc, *3 dc in next ch-1 sp. Rep from * to end, 3 dc in last dc. Ch 3, turn. 24 (27, 29, 32, 35, 35) 3-dc shells.

Row 9 (9, 9, 11, 11, 13) Sk 1 dc, (dc, ch 1, dc) in next dc, *sk 2 dc, (dc, ch 1, dc) in next dc. Rep from * to end, dc in last dc. Ch 3, turn. 24 (27, 29, 32, 35, 35) ch-1 sps plus 2 dc.

Row 10 (10, 10, 12, 12, 14) Rep Row 8 (8, 8, 10, 10, 12). 26 (29, 31, 34, 37, 37) 3-dc shells.

Rep Rows 9–10 until Front measures same as Back. 36 (41, 43, 44, 47, 47) 3-dc shells.

Note: If your row gauge is significantly different from the given pattern gauge, your number of shells may vary. It doesn't matter much—if you have more shells your cowl will drape more; if you have fewer shells it will drape less.

LEFT SHOULDER

Rep Right Shoulder instructions from Back.

RIGHT SHOULDER

Beg in 5th (5th, 6th, 6th, 6th, 7th) shell from end of row, rep instructions for Left Shoulder of Back.

Sleeve (Make 2)

Loosely ch 46 (46, 46, 46, 52, 52).

Rep Rows 1–4 of Back. 14 (14, 14, 14, 16, 16) 3-dc shells plus 2 dc.

Row 5 2 dc in 1st dc, *3 dc in next ch-1 sp. Rep from * to end, 3 dc in last dc. Ch 3, turn. 16 (16, 16, 16, 18, 18) 3-dc shells.

Row 6 Sk 1 dc, (dc, ch 1, dc) in next dc, *sk 2 dc, (dc, ch 1, dc) in next dc. Rep from * to end, dc in last dc. Ch 3, turn. 16 (16, 16, 16, 18, 18) ch-1 sps plus 2 dc.

Row 7 Sk 1st 2 dc, (dc, ch 1, dc) in next dc (center dc of 3-dc shell), *sk 2 dc, (dc, ch 1, dc) in next dc. Rep from * to end, sk 1 dc, dc in last dc. Ch 3, turn.

Row 8 *3 dc in next ch-1 sp. Rep from * to end, dc in last dc. Ch 3, turn.

Rows 9–10 Rep Rows 5–6. 18 (18, 18, 18, 20, 20) ch-1 sps plus 2 dc.

Rep Rows 7–10 4 (5, 5, 6, 6, 6) more times. 26 (28, 28, 30, 36, 36) shells.

Work even if necessary until work measures 16 (16½, 17, 18, 18, 18) in. or desired length to underarm, ending with an even-numbered row.

SLEEVE CAP SHAPING

Rep Rows 1–9 of Armhole Shaping of Back, ch 1, turn after Row 9. 16 (16, 14, 16, 20, 20) shells.

Row 10 Sl st in each of 1st 8 dc, ch 3, *sk 2 dc, (dc, ch 1, dc) in next dc. Rep from * until 3 shells remain, sk 2 sc, dc in next dc. Ch 3, turn. 12 (12, 10, 12, 16, 16) ch-1 sps.

Row 11 Sl st across to 2nd ch-1 sp, ch 3, *3 dc in next ch-1 sp. Rep from * across until 3 ch-1 sps remain, dc in next dc. Ch 3, turn. 10 (10, 8, 10, 14, 14) 3-dc shells plus 2 dc.

Row 12 Rep Row 10. 6 (6, 4, 6, 10, 10) 3-dc shells. End off.

Assembly

Block all pieces.

Stitch Front to Back at shoulders.

Stitch Sleeves into place in armhole opening.

Stitch Front to Back at sides and underarm seam of Sleeve all in one seam.

Weave in all ends.

Optional: Work 1 row of sl st across only the Back neckline to prevent it from stretching out with wear.

Curvy Cowl-Neck Pullover Schematics

BACK

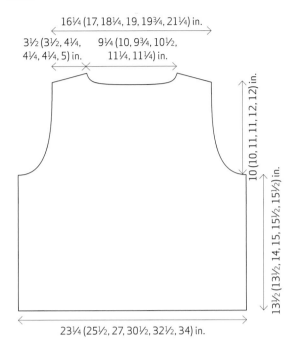

16¼ (17, 18¼, 19, 19¾, 21¼) in.

3½ (3½, 4¼, 4¼, 4¼, 5) in.

9¼ (10, 9¾, 10½, 11¼, 11¼) in.

10 (10, 11, 11, 12, 12) in.

13½ (13½, 14, 15, 15½, 15½) in.

23¼ (25½, 27, 30½, 32½, 34) in.

SLEEVE

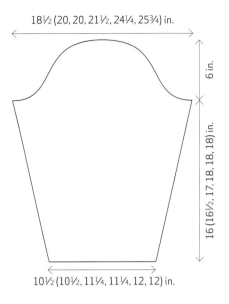

18½ (20, 20, 21½, 24¼, 25¾) in.

6 in.

16 (16½, 17, 18, 18, 18) in.

10½ (10½, 11¼, 11¼, 12, 12) in.

FRONT

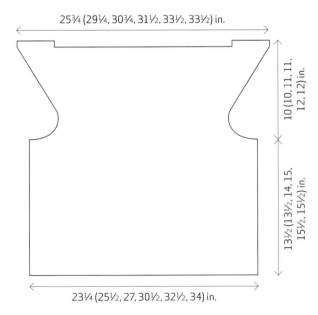

25¾ (29¼, 30¾, 31½, 33½, 33½) in.

10 (10, 11, 11, 12, 12) in.

13½ (13½, 14, 15, 15½, 15½) in.

23¼ (25½, 27, 30½, 32½, 34) in.

Verdant Pullover

Neckline details are a terrific way to draw attention to your face, right where you want it! The set-in collar pieces embellished with spike stitches in contrasting colors are a perfect match to the cuffs, and the simple main stitch pattern gives an allover texture to the sweater that is attractive and easy to wear.

Tip: If the decorative spike stitches aren't your style, you can make the collar and cuff insets in simple single crochet to accentuate the textural difference.

SKILL LEVEL
Intermediate

FINISHED BUST
L (XL, 2X, 3X, 4X, 5X); 44 (48, 53½, 57½, 61, 65) in.

YARN
Caron® Spa; 11 (12, 13, 14, 15, 16) skeins Dark Driftwood, #0013 (Color A) and 1 skein each Naturally, #0007 (Color B) and Greensleeves, #0009 (Color C) (3 oz/251 yds); 3,263 (3,514, 3,765, 4,016, 4,267, 4,518) yds worsted weight yarn (CYCA 4, Medium, see p. 146)

NOTIONS
Hook size G/6 U.S. (4 mm) *or size needed to obtain gauge*
Tapestry needle

GAUGE
17 sts and 14 rows = 4 in. in patt st for body; 18 sts and 20 rows = 4 in. in sc

NOTE
Ch-2 counts as hdc throughout.

SPECIAL STITCHES
Spike Cluster: Insert hook 2 sts back and 1 row below the indicated st, yo, pull through work loosely; insert hook 1 st back and 2 rows below the indicated st, yo, pull through work loosely; insert hook 3 rows directly below indicated st, yo, pull through work loosely; insert hook 1 st forward and 2 rows below indicated st, yo, pull through work loosely; insert hook 2 sts forward and 1 row below indicated st, yo, pull through work loosely; yo, pull through all loops on hook, ch 1 to tighten cluster.

Back

With Color A, ch 121 (129, 137, 149, 157, 165).
Row 1 Sc in 2nd ch from hook and in each ch across. 120 (128, 136, 148, 156, 164) sc. Ch 2, turn.
Row 2 *Sk 1 sc, 2 hdc in next sc. Rep from * to end, hdc in last sc. Ch 1, turn. 59 (63, 67, 73, 77, 81) 2-hdc shells plus 2 hdc.
Row 3 Sc in each hdc across. Ch 2, turn.
Rows 4–6 Rep Rows 2–3, then Row 2 once more.
Row 7 Sc2tog, sc in each hdc across to last 2 sts, sc2tog. Ch 2, turn. 118 (126, 134, 146, 154, 162) sc.
Row 8 1 hdc, *sk 1 sc, 2 hdc in next sc. Rep from * until 2 sts remain, hdc in each of last 2 sc. Ch 1, turn. 58 (62, 66, 72, 76, 80) 2-hdc shells plus 4 hdc.
Row 9 Sc in each hdc across. Ch 2, turn.
Row 10 Rep Row 8.
Row 11 Rep Row 7. 116 (124, 132, 144, 152, 160) sc.

continued on page 30

Row 12 Rep Row 2. 57 (61, 65, 71, 75, 79) 2-hdc shells plus 2 hdc.

Rows 13–14 Rep Row 3, then Row 2.

Rep Rows 7–14 for pattern until 94 (102, 114, 122, 130, 138) sc remain, ending with a Row 13. Work even if necessary by alternating Rows 2 and 3, until work measures 17 (17, 18, 18, 19, 19) in. from beg, ending with a Row 2.

ARMHOLE SHAPING

Row 1 Sl st in each of 8 (9, 11, 9, 11, 11) sts, ch 1, sc in each st across until 8 (9, 11, 9, 11, 11) sts rem, ch 3, turn. 78 (84, 92, 104, 108, 116) sc.

Row 2 Rep Row 2 of Back.

Row 3 Sl st in 1st st, sc2tog, sc in each sc across until 3 sts remain, sc2tog, leave last st unworked. Ch 3, turn. 74 (80, 88, 100, 104, 112) sc.

Row 4 Rep Row 2 of Back.

Rows 5–8 (8, 10, 14, 14, 16) Rep Rows 3–4. 66 (72, 76, 80, 84, 88) sc.

Work even on these sts (rep Rows 2–3 of Back) until work measures 6½ (7, 7¼, 8, 8¼, 8¼) in. from start of Armhole Shaping, ending with a Row 2.

Collar Cut-Out

FIRST SIDE

Row 1 Sc in each of 1st 8 (10, 12, 14, 16, 18) sts. Ch 2, turn.

Row 2 *Sk 1 sc, 2 hdc in next sc. Rep from * to end, hdc in last sc. Ch 1, turn. 3 (4, 5, 6, 7, 8) 2-hdc shells plus 2 hdc.

Rep Rows 1–2 until work measures 9½ (10, 10¼, 11, 11¼, 11¼) in. from start of Armhole Shaping. End off.

SECOND SIDE

Rep First Side instructions on the last 10 (12, 12, 14, 16, 18) sts of final row of Armhole Shaping instructions.

Front

Rep instructions for Back until work measures 2½ (3, 3¼, 4, 4¼, 4¼) in. from start of Armhole Shaping, ending with a Row 2.

Rep instructions for Collar Cut-Out.

Sleeve (Make 2)

CUFF

With Color A, ch 116 (122, 126, 132, 136, 142).

Row 1 (RS) Sc in 2nd ch from hook and in each ch across. 115 (121, 125, 131, 135, 141) sc.

Rows 2–4 Sc in each sc across, ch 1, turn.

Row 5 Change to Color B, 2 sc in 1st sc, sc in each of next 2 (2, 1, 1, 3, 1) sc, spike cluster (see Special Stitches) in next sc, *sc in each of next 5 sc, spike cluster in next sc. Rep from * to last 3 (3, 2, 2, 4, 2) sts, sc in each of next 2 (2, 1, 1, 3, 1) sc, 2 sc in last sc. Ch 1, turn. 117 (123, 127, 133, 136, 143) sc.

Rows 6–8 Sc in each sc across. Ch 1, turn.

Row 9 Change to Color C, sc in each of 1st 7 (7, 6, 6, 8, 6) sc, spike cluster in next sc, * sc in each of next 5 sc, spike cluster in next sc. Rep from * to last 7 (7, 6, 6, 8, 6) sts, sc to end. Ch 1, turn.

Rows 10–12 Sc in each sc across. Ch 1, turn.

Rows 13 Change to Color A, 2 sc in 1st sc, sc in each of next 3 (3, 2, 2, 4, 2) sc, spike cluster in next sc, *sc in each of next 5 sc, spike cluster in next sc. Rep from * to last 3 (3, 2, 2, 4, 2) sts, sc to last st, 2 sc in last sc. Ch 1, turn. 119 (125, 127, 135, 138, 145) sc.

Rows 14–15 With Color A, rep Rows 6–7. End off. Turn work 180 degrees to work Row 1 of the Sleeve Proper on the opposite side of the starting ch of the cuff.

SLEEVE PROPER

Row 1 With Color A, 114 (120, 124, 130, 134, 140) sc evenly across opposite side of starting chain.

Row 2 *Sk 1 sc, 2 hdc in next sc. Rep from * to end, hdc in last sc. Ch 1, turn. 56 (59, 61, 64, 66, 69) 2-hdc shells plus 2 hdc.

Row 3 Sc in each hdc across. Ch 2, turn.

Row 4–6 Rep Rows 2–3, then Row 2 once more.

Row 7 Sc2tog, sc in each hdc across to last 2 sts, sc2tog. Ch 2, turn. 112 (118, 122, 128, 132, 138) sc.

Row 8 1 hdc, *sk 1 sc, 2 hdc in next sc. Rep from * until 2 sts rem, hdc in each of last 2 sc. Ch 1, turn.

Row 9 Sc2tog, sc in each hdc across to last 2 sts, sc2tog. Ch 2, turn. 110 (116, 120, 126, 130, 136) sc.

Row 10 Rep Row 2.

Rows 11–26 (26, 26, 26, 26, 28) Rep Rows 7–10. 74 (80, 84, 90, 94, 96) sts.

Work straight without shaping in established pattern till sleeve measures 17½ (17½, 18, 18, 18½, 18½) in. from bottom edge of cuff, ending with an even row.

SLEEVE CAP

Row 1 Sl st in each of 8 (9, 11, 9, 11, 11) sts, ch 1, sc in each st across until 8 (9, 11, 9, 11, 11) sts rem, ch 3, turn. 58 (62, 62, 72, 72, 74) sts.

Row 2 Work 2-hdc shell row across as established.

continued on page 32

The spike stitch collars and cuffs are completed separately, then turned upside down so the "spikes" point upward, toward the face. Be sure to work your first row of single crochets in the bump or back of the chain for ease of assembly later.

Row 3 Sl st in 1st st, sc2tog, sc in each sc across until 3 sts remain, sc2tog, leave last st unworked. Ch 2, turn. 54 (58, 58, 68, 68, 70) sc.

Row 4 Work 2-hdc shell row across as established.

Rep Rows 3–4 until 10 (14, 14, 20, 20, 22) sts remain after a Row 3.

Front Collar

SIDE PIECE 1

With Color C, ch 9.

Row 1 Sc in 2nd ch from hook and in each ch across. 8 sc.

Rows 2–4 Sc in each sc across, ch 1, turn.

Row 5 Change to Color B, sc in each of 1st 2 sc, spike cluster in next sc, sc in each sc to end. Ch 1, turn.

Rows 6–8 Sc in each sc across. Ch 1, turn.

Row 9 Change to Color A, sc in each of 1st 5 sc, spike cluster in next sc, sc in each sc to end. Ch 1, turn.

Rows 10–12 Sc in each sc across. Ch 1, turn.

Rows 13–16 Change to Color C, rep Rows 5–8.

Rows 17–20 Change to Color B, rep Rows 9–12. Do not end off, set aside.

SIDE PIECE 2

Rep Rows 1–4 of Side Piece 1.

Row 5 Change to Color B, rep Row 9 of Side Piece 1.

Rows 6–8 Rep Rows 6–8 of Side Piece 1.

Row 9 Change to Color A, rep Row 5 of Side Piece 1.

Rows 10–12 Rep Rows 10–12 of Side Piece 1.

Row 13 Change to Color C, rep Row 9 of Side Piece 1.

Rows 14–16 Rep Rows 6–8 of Side Piece 1.

Rows 17–20 Change to Color B, rep Rows 5–8. Do not end off, set aside.

COLLAR ASSEMBLY

Begin stitching with Side Piece 1.

Row 1 With Color A, sc in each of 1st 2 sc, spike cluster in next sc, sc in each of next 5 sc, ch 37 loosely; working across Side Piece 2, sc in each of 1st 6 sc, spike cluster in next sc, sc in each sc to end. Ch 1, turn.

Rows 2–4 Sc in each sc across. Ch 1, turn.

Row 5 With Color C, sc in each of 1st 5 sc, spike cluster in next sc, *sc in each of next 5 sc, spike cluster in next sc. Rep from * to end, sc in each sc to end. Ch 1, turn.

Rows 6–8 Sc in each sc across. Ch 1, turn.

Row 9 Change to Color B, sc in each of 1st 2 sc, spike cluster in next sc, * sc in each of next 5 sc, spike cluster in next sc. Rep from * across, sc in each sc to end. Ch 1, turn.

Rows 10–12 Sc in each sc across. Ch 1, turn.

Rows 13–15 Change to Color A, rep Rows 5–7. End off.

Back Collar

Rep Rows 1–8 of Side Piece 1 and Side Piece 2 instructions, then rep all of Collar Assembly instructions.

Assembly

Sew Front Collar into Front neck opening, using a whip st in Color A.

Sew Back Collar into Back neck opening, using a whip st in Color A.

Work 1 rnd sc in Color A around entire neck opening.

Sew Front to Back at shoulders.

Sew Sleeves into place.

Sew side and sleeve underarm seams all at once.

Weave in all ends.

Verdant Pullover Schematics

BODY

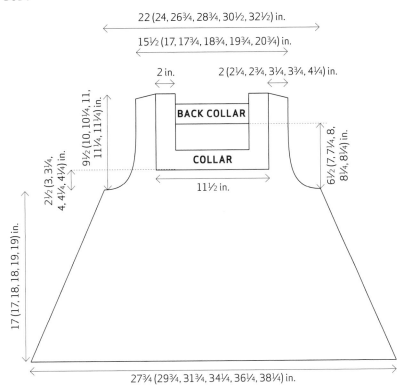

22 (24, 26¾, 28¾, 30½, 32½) in.

15½ (17, 17¾, 18¾, 19¾, 20¾) in.

2 in.

2 (2¼, 2¾, 3¼, 3¾, 4¼) in.

BACK COLLAR

COLLAR

9½ (10, 10¼, 11, 11¼, 11¼) in.

2½ (3, 3¼, 4, 4¼, 4¼) in.

6½ (7, 7¼, 8, 8¼, 8¼) in.

11½ in.

17 (17, 18, 18, 19, 19) in.

27¾ (29¾, 31¾, 34¼, 36¼, 38¼) in.

SLEEVE

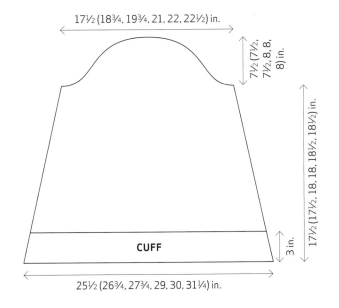

17½ (18¾, 19¾, 21, 22, 22½) in.

7½ (7½, 7½, 8, 8, 8) in.

17½ (17½, 18, 18, 18½, 18½) in.

3 in.

CUFF

25½ (26¾, 27¾, 29, 30, 31¼) in.

continued on page 34

Verdant Pullover Body Stitch Diagram

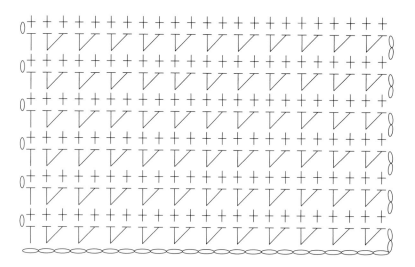

Verdant Pullover Spike Stitch Diagram

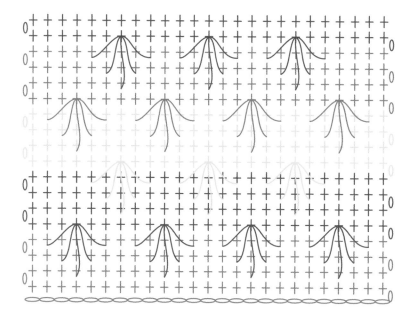

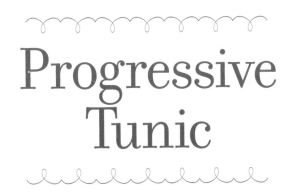

Progressive Tunic

The Progressive Tunic uses three contrasting shades of lace-weight yarn, held together and changed out one strand at a time, to create a shaded fabric from hem to shoulder. It is a great layering piece to add some interest to everyday wardrobe items, and the fine wool yarn makes the finished garment light in weight, even when stitching with multiple strands. Use neutrals as I did here, or go with funky colors if that is more your style!

Tip: While I chose to change out a strand of yarn on a regular basis, your stripes don't have to march up the garment in regiments if you don't want them to. Change out a strand of yarn at random, or try repeating small stripes for a different look.

SKILL LEVEL
Easy

FINISHED BUST
L (XL, 2X, 3X, 4X, 5X); 44½ (48, 52½, 58½, 62, 66½) in.

YARN
Filatura Di Crosa Nirvana; 5 (6, 6, 7, 7, 8) skeins each Dark Chocolate, #16 (Color A); Camel, #13 (Color B); and Natural, #11 (Color C) (25 g/372 yds); 5,580 (6,696, 6,696, 7,812, 7,812, 8,928) yds lace weight yarn (CYCA 0, Lace, see p. 146)

NOTIONS
Hook size F/5 U.S. (3.75 mm) *or size needed to obtain gauge*
3 stitch markers
Tapestry needle

GAUGE
Nine 3-sc shells (27 sc) and 20 rows = 4 in. in patt st

Back

With 3 strands of Color A, loosely ch 162 (174, 189, 210, 222, 237).
Row 1 3 sc in 3rd ch from hook, *sk 2 ch, 3 sc in next ch. Rep from * to end. Ch 1, turn. 54 (58, 63, 70, 74, 79) 3-sc shells.
Row 2 Sk 1st sc, 3 sc in next sc, *sk 2 sc, 3 sc in next sc. Rep from * to end. Ch 1, turn.
Rep Row 2 for pattern until 20 rows are complete.
With 2 strands Color A and 1 strand Color B, rep Row 2 until 20 more rows are complete.

DECREASE

Row 1 With 1 strand Color A and 2 strands Color B, sk 1st sc, 2 sc in next sc, *sk 2 sc, 3 sc in next sc. Rep from * until 4 sc remain, sk 2 sc, 2 sc in next sc. Ch 1, turn. 52 (56, 61, 68, 72, 77) 3-sc shells plus 2 2-sc shells.
Rows 2-4 2 sc in 1st sc, *sk 2 sc, 3 sc in next sc. Rep from * until 3 sc remain, sk 2 sc, 2 sc in next sc. Ch 1, turn.
Row 5 Sc in 1st sc, *sk 2 sc, 3 sc in next sc. Rep from * until 3 sc remain, sk 2 sc, sc in next sc. Ch 1, turn. 52 (56, 61, 68, 72, 77) 3-sc shells plus 2 sc.
Rows 6-8 Sc in 1st sc, sk 1 sc, 3 sc in next sc, *sk 2 sc, 3 sc in next sc. Rep from * until 2 sc remain, sk 1 sc, sc in next sc.
Row 9 Sl st in 1st sc, sk 1 sc, 3 sc in next sc, *sk 2 sc, 3 sc in next sc. Rep from * until 2 sc remain, ch 1, turn. 52 (56, 61, 68, 72, 77) 3-sc shells.

continued on page 36

Rows 10–12 Sk 1st sc, 3 sc in next sc, *sk 2 sc, 3 sc in next sc. Rep from * to end. Ch 1, turn.

Rows 13–20 Rep Rows 1–8. 50 (54, 59, 66, 70, 75) 3-sc shells plus 2 sc.

Row 21 With 3 strands of Color B, rep Row 9. 50 (54, 59, 66, 70, 75) 3-sc shells.

WORK EVEN

Rows 1–19 Sk 1st sc, 3 sc in next sc, *sk 2 sc, 3 sc in next sc. Rep from * to end. Ch 1, turn.

With 2 strands Color B and 1 strand Color C, rep Row 1 15 times.

ARMHOLE SHAPING

Row 1 Continuing with color as established, sl st in next sc, (ch 1, sk 2, sc, sl st in next sc) 3 (3, 4, 4, 5, 6) times, *sk 2 sc, 3 sc in next sc. Rep from * until 4 (4, 5, 5, 6, 7) 3-sc shells remain. Ch 1, turn. 42 (46, 49, 56, 58, 61) 3-sc shells.

Row 2 Sk 1st sc, 2 sc in next sc, *sk 2 sc, 3 sc in next sc. Rep from * until 4 sc remain, sk 2 sc, 2 sc in next sc. Ch 1, turn. 40 (44, 47, 54, 56, 59) 3-sc shells plus 2 2-sc shells.

Row 3 2 sc in 1st sc, *sk 2 sc, 3 sc in next sc. Rep from * until 3 sc remain, sk 2 sc, 2 sc in next sc. Ch 1, turn.

Row 4 Sc in 1st sc, *sk 2 sc, 3 sc in next sc. Rep from * until 3 sc remain, sk 2 sc, sc in next sc. Ch 1, turn. 40 (44, 47, 54, 56, 59) 3-sc shells plus 2 sc.

Row 5 Sc in 1st sc, sk 1 sc, 3 sc in next sc, *sk 2 sc, 3 sc in next sc. Rep from * until 2 sc remain, sk 1 sc, sc in next sc. Ch 1, turn.

Row 6 With 1 strand Color B and 2 strands Color C, sl st in 1st sc, sk 1 sc, 3 sc in next sc, *sk 2 sc, 3 sc in next sc. Rep from * until 2 sc remain, ch 1, turn. 40 (44, 47, 54, 56, 59) 3-sc shells.

Rows 7–8 Sk 1st sc, 3 sc in next sc, *sk 2 sc, 3 sc in next sc. Rep from * to end. Ch 1, turn.

Rows 9–15 Rep Rows 2–8. 38 (42, 45, 52, 54, 57) 3-sc shells.

Sizes L and XL only:
Go to Work Even below.

Sizes 2X (3X, 4X, 5X) only:
Change to 3 strands Color C when 20 rows have been completed in the previous gradation.
Rep Rows 2–8 1 (3, 4, 5) time(s). 43 (46, 46, 47) 3-sc shells.

WORK EVEN (ALL SIZES)
Work even by repeating Row 8, changing to 3 strands of Color C when 20 rows have been completed in the

previous gradation, or until work measures 9½ (10, 10½, 11, 11½, 12) in. from the start of Armhole Shaping.

FIRST SHOULDER

Row 1 Sk 1 sc, sl st in next sc, (ch 1, sk 2 sc, sl st in next sc) 2 (2, 3, 3, 4, 4) times, *sk 2 sc, 3 sc in next sc. Rep from * 7 times. Ch 1, turn.

Row 2 Sk 1 sc, 3 sc in next sc, *sk 2 sc, 3 sc in next sc. Rep from * 3 times. Ch 1, turn. 5 3-sc shells.

Row 3 Sk 1 sc, sl sc in next sc, ch 1, sk 2 sc, sl st in next sc, *sk2 sc, 3 sc in next sc. Rep from * to end. Ch 1, turn. 3 3-sc shells.

SECOND SHOULDER

Row 1 Working in same direction as Row 1 of First Shoulder, sk 18 (22, 21, 24, 22, 23) 3-dc shells, sk 1 sc, 3 sc in next sc, *sk 2 sc, 3 sc in next sc. Rep from * 6 times. Ch 1, turn. 7 3-sc shells.

Row 2 Sk 1 sc, sl st in next sc, ch 1, sk 2 sc, sl st in next sc, *sk 2 sc, 3 sc in next sc. Rep from * to end. 5 3-sc shells.

Row 3 Sk 1 sc, 3 sc in next sc, (sk 2 sc, 3 sc in next sc) 2 times. 3 3-sc shells.

Front
Rep instructions for Back until Row 11 of Armhole Shaping is completed.

Divide for neckline:
Place a stitch marker in the center shell of the last row completed, or between two shells if you have an even number. Mark the 8th (8th, 8th, 10th, 10th, 10th) shell on either side of the center marker.

LEFT FRONT

Row 1 Sc in 1st sc, sk 1 sc, 3 sc in next sc, *sk 2 sc, 3 sc in next sc. Rep from * to shell before 1st marker. Ch 1, turn. 24 (28, 30, 28, 40, 42) 3-sc shells plus 1 sc.

Row 2 Sk 1 sc, 3 sc in next sc, *sk 2 sc, 3 sc in next sc. Rep from * until 2 sc remain, ch 1, turn. 24 (28, 30, 28, 40, 42) 3-sc shells.

Rows 3–4 Sk 1st sc, 3 sc in next sc, *sk 2 sc, 3 sc in next sc. Rep from * to end. Ch 1, turn.

Sizes L and XL only:
Go to Work Even on p. 38.

Sizes 2X (3X, 4X, 5X) only:
Row 5 Sk 1st sc, 2 sc in next sc, *sk 2 sc, 3 sc in next sc. Rep from * to end. Ch 1, turn. 28 (26, 38, 40) 3-sc shells plus 2 2-sc shells.

continued on page 38

Row 6 Sk 1st sc, 3 sc in next sc, *sk 2 sc, 3 sc in next sc. Rep from * until 3 sc remain, sk 2 sc, 2 sc in next sc. Ch 1, turn.

Row 7 Sc in 1st sc, *sk 2 sc, 3 sc in next sc. Rep from * to end. Ch 1, turn. 28 (26, 38, 40) 3-sc shells plus 2 sc.

Size 2X only:

Rep Rows 1–2. Go to Work Even below.

Sizes 3X (4X, 5X) only:

Rep Rows 1–7 2 (3, 4) times, then rep Rows 1–2 once. 43 (46, 47) 3-sc shells.

WORK EVEN (ALL SIZES)

Work even by repeating Row 8 of Back, changing to 3 strands of Color C when 20 rows have been completed

The Progressive Tunic graduates from dark to light colors, but you can play around with the color changes. Keep in mind that darker colors minimize, and brighter, lighter colors draw the eye.

in the previous gradation, until work measures 9½ (10, 10½, 11, 11½, 12) in. from the start of Armhole Shaping.

LEFT SHOULDER

Rep instructions for Left Shoulder of Back.

RIGHT FRONT

Row 1 Sc in 1st sc, sk 1 sc, 3 sc in next sc, *sk 2 sc, 3 sc in next sc. Rep from * to shell before 1st marker. Ch 1, turn. 24 (28, 30, 28, 40, 42) 3-sc shells plus 1 sc.

Row 2 Sk 1 sc, 3 sc in next sc, *sk 2 sc, 3 sc in next sc. Rep from * until 2 sc remain, ch 1, turn. 24 (28, 30, 28, 40, 42) 3-sc shells.

Rows 3–4 Sk 1st sc, 3 sc in next sc, *sk 2 sc, 3 sc in next sc. Rep from * to end. Ch 1, turn.

Sizes L and XL only:

Go to Work Even below.

Sizes 2X (3X, 4X, 5X) only:

Row 5 Sk 1st sc, 2 sc in next sc, *sk 2 sc, 3 sc in next sc. Rep from * to end. Ch 1, turn. 28 (26, 38, 40) 3-sc shells plus 2 2-sc shells.

Row 6 Sk 1st sc, 3 sc in next sc, *sk 2 sc, 3 sc in next sc. Rep from * until 3 sc remain, sk 2 sc, 2 sc in next sc. Ch 1, turn.

Row 7 Sc in 1st sc, *sk 2 sc, 3 sc in next sc. Rep from * to end. Ch 1, turn. 28 (26, 38, 40) 3-sc shells plus 2 sc.

Size 2X only:

Rep Rows 1–2. Go to Work Even below.

Sizes 3X (4X, 5X) only:

Rep Rows 1–7 2 (3, 4) times, then rep Rows 1–2 once more. 43 (46, 47) 3-sc shells.

WORK EVEN

Work even by repeating Row 8 of Back, changing to 3 strands Color C when 20 rows have been completed in the previous gradation if you haven't already, until work measures 9½ (10, 10½, 11, 11½, 12) in. from start of Armhole Shaping.

RIGHT SHOULDER

Rep instructions for Right Shoulder of Back.

Assembly

This stitch is very stretchy and does not need a hard blocking.

Sew the front to the back at the side seams and shoulders. Weave in all ends.

Progressive Tunic Schematic

FRONT AND BACK

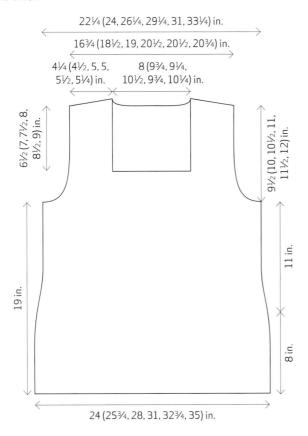

22¼ (24, 26¼, 29¼, 31, 33¼) in.

16¾ (18½, 19, 20½, 20½, 20¾) in.

4¼ (4½, 5, 5, 5½, 5¼) in.

8 (9¾, 9¼, 10½, 9¾, 10¼) in.

6½ (7, 7½, 8, 8½, 9) in.

9½ (10, 10½, 11, 11½, 12) in.

11 in.

19 in.

8 in.

24 (25¾, 28, 31, 32¾, 35) in.

Progressive Tunic Stitch Diagram

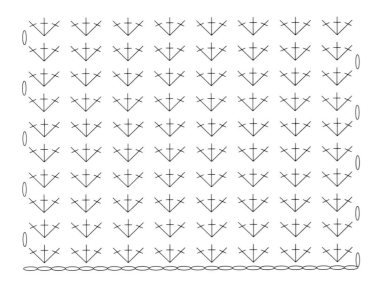

Counterpoint Pullover

High contrast doesn't have to be all about color. The lace stitch sleeves in this sweater are a strong counterpoint to the solid stitch pattern that makes up the sweater's body. This will be a go-to piece in your wardrobe that you can dress up or down.

Tip: Change the angle of the bell sleeve by changing the number of starting chains in a multiple of 8 chains. If you narrow the sleeve hem, you will need less decrease; if you make it wider, you will need more—just make sure you end up with the number of stitches you should have right before the Armhole Shaping begins.

SKILL LEVEL
Intermediate

FINISHED BUST
L (XL, 2X 3X, 4X, 5X); 46 (50, 54, 60, 64, 68) in.

YARN
Caron Country; 9 (10, 10, 11, 12, 13) skeins Deep Purple, #0014 (3 oz/185 yds); 1,665 (1,850, 1,850, 2,035, 2,220, 2,405) yds worsted weight yarn (CYCA 4, Medium, see p. 146)

NOTIONS
Hook size I/9 U.S. (5.5 mm) *or size needed to obtain gauge*
Tapestry needle

GAUGE
12 sts and 10 rows = 4 in. in hdc; 18 sts (3 ch-5 sps) and 5 rows = 4 in. in patt st for sleeves

NOTES
Ch-2 counts as 1 hdc throughout.
Ch-3 counts as 1 dc throughout.
Ch-5 counts as 1 sc plus ch-2 throughout.

Back
Ch 70 (76, 82, 91, 97, 103).
Row 1 Hdc in 3rd ch from hook and in each ch across. Ch 2, turn. 69 (75, 81, 90, 96, 102) hdc.
Row 2 Hdc in each hdc across. Ch 2, turn.
Rep Row 2 for pattern until work measures 3 (3, 3, 4, 4, 4) in. from beg.

WAIST SHAPING
Row 1 Hdc2tog, hdc in each hdc to last 2 sts, hdc2tog. Ch 2, turn. 67 (73, 79, 88, 94, 100) hdc.
Row 2 Hdc in each hdc across. Ch 2, turn.
Rows 3–6 Rep Rows 1–2 twice. 63 (69, 75, 84, 90, 96) hdc after Row 6.
Row 7 2 hdc in 1st hdc, dc in each hdc across to last hdc, 2 hdc in last hdc. Ch 2, turn. 65 (71, 77, 86, 92, 100) hdc.
Row 8 Rep Row 2.
Rows 9–12 Rep Rows 7–8 twice. 69 (75, 81, 90, 96, 104) hdc. End of waist shaping.
Work even in hdc until work measures 15¾ (15¾, 16¼, 17¼, 17¾, 17¾) in., ch 1 to turn at end of last row.

ARMHOLE SHAPING
Row 1 Sl st in each of 1st 4 (4, 5, 6, 6, 7) sts, ch 2, hdc in next hdc and in each hdc across until 3 (3, 4, 5, 5, 6) sts remain. Ch 2, turn. 63 (69, 73, 80, 86, 92) hdc.
Row 2 Hdc2tog, hdc across to last 2 sts, hdc2tog. Ch 2, turn. 61 (67, 71, 78, 84, 90) hdc.
Rows 3–4 Rep Row 2. 57 (63, 67, 74, 80, 86) hdc.

continued on page 42

Sizes L (XL, 2X, 3X) only:
Row 5 Hdc in each hdc across.
Row 6 Rep Row 2. 55 (61, 65, 72) hdc.
Rep Rows 5–6 2 (3, 4, 5) times. 51 (55, 57, 62) hdc.
Work even on these sts if necessary until work measures
9½ (10, 10½, 11) in. from start of Armhole Shaping.
Ch 1, turn at end of last row. Go to Shoulder Shaping.

Sizes 4X and 5X only:
Rows 5–6 (8) Rep Row 2. 76 (78) hdc.
Row 7 (9) Hdc in each hdc across.
Row 8 (10) Rep Row 2. 74 (76) hdc.
Rep Rows 7–8 (9–10) 5 times. 64 (66) hdc.
Work even on these sts if necessary until work measures 11½ (12) in. from start of Armhole Shaping. Ch 1, turn at end of last row.

Shoulder Shaping

RIGHT SHOULDER
Row 1 (RS) Hdc in each of 1st 12 (12, 13, 14, 15, 15) hdc. Ch 2, turn.
Row 2 (WS) Hdc in each of 1st 7 (7, 8, 9, 8, 8) hdc, sc in each of next 1 (1, 1, 1, 2, 2) hdc, sl st in next hdc. Ch 1, turn. 9 (9, 10, 11, 11, 11) sts.
Row 3 Sl st in each of 1st 4 sts, sc in each of next 1 (1, 1, 2, 2, 2) hdc, hdc in each of next 4 (4, 5, 5, 5, 5) hdc. End off. 6 (6, 7, 8, 8, 8) sts.

LEFT SHOULDER
Row 1 (RS) Working in same direction as Row 1 of Right Shoulder, sk 27 (31, 31, 34, 34, 38) hdc for neckline, hdc in each of last 12 (12, 13, 14, 15, 15) hdc. Ch 1, turn.
Row 2 (WS) Sl st in each of 1st 4 hdc, sc in each of next 1 (1, 1, 1, 2, 2) hdc, hdc in each of next 7 (7, 8, 9, 8, 8) hdc. Ch 2, turn. 9 (9, 10, 11, 11, 11) sts.
Row 3 Hdc in each of 1st 4 (4, 5, 5, 5, 5) hdc, sc in each of next 1 (1, 1, 2, 2, 2) hdc, sl st in next hdc. End off. 6 (6, 7, 8, 8, 8) sts.

Front

Work as for Back until 6 (6, 8, 10, 10, 10) rows of Armhole Shaping are complete. 55 (61, 63, 68, 72, 76) sts.

RIGHT FRONT
Row 1 (WS) Hdc in each of 1st 20 (21, 23, 24, 25, 26) hdc. Ch 2, turn.
Row 2 (RS) Hdc2tog, hdc in each hdc across to last 2 sts, hdc2tog. Ch 2, turn. 18 (19, 21, 22, 23, 24) hdc.
Row 3 Hdc in each hdc across. Ch 2, turn.

Rows 4–9 Rep Rows 2–3. 12 (13, 15, 16, 17, 18) hdc after Row 9.

Size L only:
Go to Work Even.

Sizes XL (2X, 3X, 4X, 5X) only:
Row 10 Hdc in each hdc across to last 2 scs, hdc2tog. Ch 2, turn. 12 (14, 15, 16, 17) hdc.
Row 11 Hdc in each hdc across. Ch 2, turn. Size XL only, go to Work Even.
Rows 12–13 Rep Rows 10–11. 13 (14, 15, 16) hdc. Sizes 2X (3X, 4X) only, go to Work Even.
Rows 14–15 Rep Rows 10–11.

WORK EVEN (ALL SIZES)
Work even on these sts (hdc in each hdc across) if necessary until work measures 9¾ (10¼, 10¾, 11¼, 11¾, 12¼) in. from start of Armhole Shaping, ending with a RS row. Ch 1, turn at end of last row.

Shoulder Shaping
Rep Rows 2–3 of Right Shoulder of Back.

LEFT FRONT
Row 1 (WS) Working in same direction as Row 1 of Right Front, sk 15 (19, 17, 19, 22, 24) hdc for neckline, hdc in each of last 20 (21, 23, 24, 25, 26) hdc. Ch 1, turn.
Row 2 (RS) Hdc2tog, hdc in each hdc across to last 2 sts, hdc2tog. Ch 2, turn. 18 (19, 21, 22, 23, 24) hdc.
Rows 3–9 Rep Rows 3–9 of Right Front.

Size L only:
Go to Work Even.

Sizes XL (2X, 3X, 4X, 5X) only:
Row 10 Hdc2tog, hdc in each hdc across. Ch 2, turn. 12 (14, 15, 16, 17) hdc.
Row 11 Hdc in each hdc across. Ch 2, turn. Size XL only, go to Work Even.
Rows 12–13 Rep Rows 10–11. 13 (14, 15, 16) hdc. Sizes 2X, (3X, 4X) only, go to Work Even.
Rows 14–15 Rep Rows 10–11.

WORK EVEN (ALL SIZES)
Rep Work Even instructions of Right Front.

Shoulder Shaping
Rep Rows 2–3 of Left Shoulder of Back.

continued on page 44

Scoop necks are incredibly comfortable and flattering. Find just the right scoop for your tastes by adding or removing rounds of single crochet.

Sleeve (Make 2)

Ch 81 (81, 89, 89, 97, 97).

Row 1 Sc in 7th ch from hook, * ch 5, sk 3 ch, sc in next ch. Rep from * until 2 ch remain, ch 2, sk 1 ch, dc in last ch. Ch 1, turn. 18 (18, 20, 20, 22, 22) ch-5 sps plus 2 ch-2 sps.

Row 2 Sc in dc, ch 3, sk 1st sc, 3 dc in next ch-5 sp, ch 3, sc in next sh-5 sp, *ch 3, 3 dc in next ch-5 sp, ch 3, sc in next ch-5 sp. Rep from * to end, ch 5, sc in sp created by t-ch. Ch 5, turn. 9 (9, 10, 10, 11, 11) 3-dc shells.

Row 3 Sk 1st sc, sc in ch-5 sp, *ch 5, sc in next ch-3 sp. Rep from * to end, ch 2, dc in last sc. Ch 1, turn.

Row 4 Sc in dc, ch 5, sk 1 sc, sc in next ch-5 sp, ch 3, 3 dc in next ch-5 sp, *ch 3, sc in next ch-5 sp, ch 3, 3 dc in next ch-5 sp. Rep from * to end, ch 3, sc in sp created by t-ch. Ch 1, turn.

Row 5 Sl st in 1st sc, sl st in next ch, sc in next ch, *ch 5, sc in next ch-3 sp. Rep from * to end. Ch 5, turn. 18 (18, 20, 20, 22, 22) ch-5 sps.

Row 6 Sc in 1st ch-5 sp, ch 5, sc in next ch-5 sp, *ch 3, 3 dc in next ch-5 sp, ch 3, sc in next ch-5 sp. Rep from * to end, ch 2, dc in last sc. Ch 1, turn.

Row 7 Sc in dc, *ch 5, sc in next ch-5 sp. Rep from * to end, placing last sc in sp created by t-ch, ch 5, turn.

Row 8 Sc in 1st ch-5 sp, *ch 3, 3 dc in next ch-5 sp, ch 3, sc in next ch-5 sp. Rep from * until 1 ch-5 sp remains, ch 5, sc in ch-5 sp, ch 2, dc in last sc. Ch 1, turn.

Row 9 Sl st in dc, sl st in next ch, sl st in sc, *ch 5, sc in next ch-5 sp. Rep from * to last sc, ch 2, dc in last sc. Ch 1, turn. 16 (16, 18, 18, 20, 20) ch-5 sps plus 2 ch-2 sps.

Rows 10–15 Rep Rows 4–9. 14 (14, 16, 16, 18, 18) ch-2 sps plus 2 ch-2 sps.

WORK EVEN

Row 1 Sc in dc, ch 5, sk 1 sc, sc in next ch-5 sp, ch 3, 3 dc in next ch-5 sp, *ch 3, sc in next ch-5 sp, ch 3, 3 dc in next ch-5 sp. Rep from * to end, ch 3, sc in sp created by t-ch. Ch 5, turn.

Row 2 Sc in 1st ch-3 sp, *ch 5, sc in next ch-3 sp. Rep from * to end, ch 2, dc in last sc. Ch 1, turn.

Row 3 Sc in dc, ch 3, sk 1st sc, 3 dc in next ch-5 sp, ch 3, sc in next ch-5 sp, *ch 3, 3 dc in next ch-5 sp, ch 3, sc in next ch-5 sp. Rep from * to end, ch 5, sc in sp created by t-ch. Ch 5, turn.

Row 4 Sk 1st sc, sc in ch-5 sp, *ch 5, sc in next ch-3 sp. Rep from * to end, ch 2, dc in last sc. Ch 1, turn.

Rep Rows 1–4 until sleeve measures 17 (17, 18, 18, 19, 19) in. or desired length from beg, ending with a Row 2.

SHAPE SLEEVE CAPS

Row 1 Sc in 1st dc, 2 sc in ch-2 sp, sc in next sc, 3 sc in ch-5 sp, ch 5, sk 1 sc, sc in next ch-5 sp, *ch 3, 3 dc in next ch-5 sp, ch 3, sc in next ch-5 sp. Rep from * to end, 2 more sc in last ch-5 sp, sc in next sc, 2 sc in ch-2 sp, sc in 3rd ch of t-ch. Ch 1, turn. 6 (6, 7, 7, 8, 8) 3-dc shells.

Row 2 Sl st in each of 7 sc, ch 5, sc in 1st ch-3 sp, *ch 5, sc in next ch-3 sp. Rep from * to end, ch 2, dc in next sc. Ch 1, turn. 12 (12, 14, 14, 16, 16) ch-5 sps plus 2 ch-2 sps.

Row 3 Sc in 1st dc, sc in ch-2 sp, ch 3, sk 1st sc, 3 dc in next ch-5 sp, ch 3, sc in next ch-5 sp, *ch 3, 3 dc in next ch-5 sp, ch 3, sc in next ch-5 sp. Rep from * to end, ch 5, sc in sp created by t-ch, sc in 3rd ch of t-ch. Ch 1, turn.

Row 4 Sl st in each of 2 sc, 3 sc in ch-5 sp, *ch 5, sc in next ch-3 sp. Rep from * to end. Ch 1, turn. 12 (12, 14, 14, 16, 16) ch-2 sps.

Row 5 Sl st in 1st sc, 3 sc in ch-5 sp, *ch 3, 3 dc in next ch-5 sp, ch 3, sc in next ch-5 sp. Rep from * to end, ch 5, sc in last ch-5 sp. Ch 1, turn.

Row 6 Sl st in 1st sc, 3 sc in ch-5 sp, *ch 5, sc in next ch-3 sp. Rep from * to end. Ch 1, turn. 10 (10, 12, 12, 14, 14) ch-2 sps.

Rows 7–12 Rep Rows 5–6 3 times. 4 (4, 6, 6, 8, 8) ch-2 sps after Row 12. End off.

Assembly

Block all pieces.

Stitch Front to Back at shoulders and side seams.

With RS together, seam the Sleeves by working 1 row of sc.

Turn Sleeves RS out and insert into sleeve openings, RS together. Working from the WS, sc sleeves into openings.

Neck Edging

Rnd 1 Attach yarn in back of neck by working 1 sc in any hdc, sc evenly around entire neck opening, join rnd with sl st to 1st sc.

Rnds 2–3 Ch 1, sc in each sc around. End off after Rnd 3. Weave in all ends.

Counterpoint Pullover Schematics

FRONT AND BACK

SLEEVE

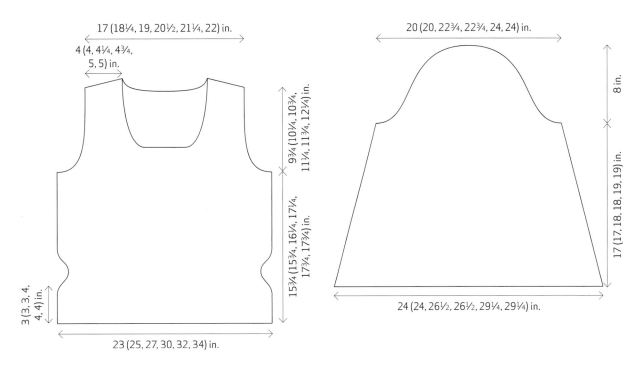

17 (18¼, 19, 20½, 21¼, 22) in.

4 (4, 4¼, 4¾, 5, 5) in.

9¾ (10¼, 10¾, 11¼, 11¾, 12¼) in.

15¾ (15¾, 16¼, 17¼, 17¾, 17¾) in.

3 (3, 3, 4, 4, 4) in.

23 (25, 27, 30, 32, 34) in.

20 (20, 22¾, 22¾, 24, 24) in.

8 in.

17 (17, 18, 18, 19, 19) in.

24 (24, 26½, 26½, 29¼, 29¼) in.

Counterpoint Pullover Lace Stitch Diagram

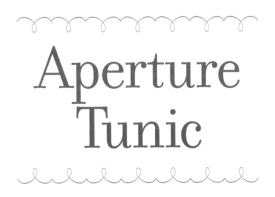

Aperture Tunic

Light and lacy, this top-down tunic will work over a tank top, a T-shirt, or even a bathing suit. Accentuate the trim by using a contrast color as shown, or make the whole sweater in one color to put the emphasis on the stitching.

DESIGNED BY KAREN RATTO WHOOLEY

Tip: Top-down construction of any pattern gives you a great opportunity to try it on as you go. Take the time to check the fit often as you stitch, so you can make any adjustments you need to make without having to rip the stitching back.

SKILL LEVEL
Intermediate

FINISHED BUST
L (XL, 2X, 3X, 4X, 5X); 47 (51, 55, 59, 63, 67) in.

YARN
Red Heart® Luster Sheen®; 3 (4, 4, 5, 5, 6) skeins Medium Blue, #0824 (MC); 1 (1, 1, 2, 2, 2) skein(s), Tea Leaf, #0615 (CC) (4 oz/335 yds); 1,340 (1,675, 1,675, 2,345, 2,345 2,680) yds sport weight yarn (CYCA 3, Light, see p. 146)

NOTIONS
Hook size F/5 U.S. (3.75 mm) *or size needed to obtain gauge*
2 stitch markers
Tapestry needle
1 button, 1 in. in diameter

GAUGE
10 dc and 9 rows = 4 in. in patt st

NOTE
3-ch turn counts as dc unless indicated otherwise.

SPECIAL STITCHES
Shell: (2 dc, ch 2, 2 dc) in st/sp indicated.
Corner: (dc, ch 2, dc) in st/sp indicated.
Sc3tog: (Insert hook in next st, yo, and bring up a loop) 3 times, yo, and pull through all 4 loops on hook.

Yoke

Ch 132.
Row 1 Sc in 6th ch from hook (counts as 1 dc plus ch-2), ch 3, sk 2 ch, sc in next ch, (ch 4, sk 3 ch, sc in next ch, ch 3, sk 2 ch, sc in next ch) 3 times, [ch 2, sk 1 ch, corner in next ch, corner in next ch, ch 2, sk 1 ch] once, rep between ( ) 9 times, rep between [ ] once, rep between ( ) 4 times, ch 2, dc in last ch. Ch 1, turn. 6 ch-2 sps, 4 corners, 2 dc, 17 ch-3 sps, 16 ch-4 sps.
Row 2 Sc in 1st dc, (shell in next ch-3 sp, sc in next ch-4 sp) 4 times, [sc in next ch-2 sp, sc in next dc, corner in next ch-2 sp, sc in next 2 dc, corner in next 2 ch-2 sps, sc in next dc, sc in next ch-2 sp], rep between ( ) 9 times, rep between [ ] once, rep between ( ) 4 times. Ch 3, turn. 17 shells, 4 corners, 30 sc.
Row 3 Dc in 1st sc, ch 1, 2 dc in shell sp, (ch 1, 2 dc in next sc, ch 1, 2 dc in next shell sp) 3 times, [2 dc in next sc, ch 1, 2 dc in next dc, ch 1, corner in ch-2 sp, ch 1, [[2 dc in next sc, ch 1]] twice, corner in ch-2 sp, ch 1, 2 dc in next dc, sk 1 sc] once, rep between ( ) 9 times, rep between [ ] once, rep between ( ) 4 times, ch 1, 2 dc in last sc. Ch 5, turn. 42 ch sps, 47 dc pairs, 4 corners.

continued on page 48

Row 4 Sc in 1st ch sp, (ch 3, sc in next ch sp, ch 4, sc in next ch sp) rep across to and in ch sp before corner, [ch 2, corner in ch-2 sp, ch 2, sc in next ch sp] once, rep between ( ) across to ch sp before corner, rep between [ ] once, rep between ( ) across to ch sp before corner, rep between [ ] once, rep between ( ) across to ch sp before corner, rep between [ ] once, rep between ( ) across to and in last ch sp, ch 2, dc in last dc. Ch 1, turn. 23 ch-3 sps, 21 ch-4 sps, 10 ch-2 sps.

Row 5 Sc in 1st ch sp, ([shell in every ch-3 sp and sc in every ch-4 sp across] to corner, sc in ch-2 sp, sc in next dc, corner in ch-2 sp, sc in next dc, sc in next ch-2 sp) 4 times, rep between [ ] to end, sc in last ch sp. Ch 3, turn. 23 shells.

Row 6 Dc in 1st sc, ch 1, ([2 dc in next shell, ch 1, 2 dc in next sc, ch 1 across] to corner, 2 dc in next dc, corner in ch-2 sp, 2 dc in next dc, ch 1, sk 1 sc, 2 dc in next sc, ch 1) 4 times, rep between [ ] to end, 2 dc in last sc. Ch 1, turn.

Rows 7–9 Rep Rows 4–6. 29 shells after Row 8.

Rows 10–12 Rep Rows 4–6. 35 shells after Row 11.

Rows 13–15 Rep Rows 4–6. 41 shells after Row 14.

BODY

Row 1 Dc in 1st sc, ch 1, *2 dc in next ch-2 sp, ch 1, (2 dc in next sc, ch 1, 2 dc in next ch-2 sp, ch 1) across to the 4 underarm sc, sk 1 sc, dc in next 2 sc, ch 1; rep from * once more, join into rnd with sl st in top of t-ch.

Note: The project is now worked in the round. Do not turn.

Rnd 2 Ch 4, sc in next ch-1 sp, *ch 3, sc in next ch-1 sp, ch 4, sc in next ch-1 sp; rep from * around, ending last rep with ch 3, sc in next ch-1 sp, sl st in same st as join of last rnd.

Rnd 3 Sc in next ch-4 sp, *shell in next ch-3 sp, sc in next ch-4 sp; rep from * across ending last rep with shell in last ch-3 sp, sl st in beg sc.

Rnd 4 Ch 4, *2 dc in next ch-2 sp, ch 1, 2 dc in next sc, ch 1; rep from * across, ending with dc in last sc, join with sl st in 3rd ch of beg ch-4.

Rnd 5 Sc in next ch-1 sp, *ch 3, sc in next ch-1 sp, ch 4, sc in next ch-1 sp; rep from * around ending with sl st in beg sc.

Rnd 6 Sl st in next ch-3 sp, ch 3, (dc, ch 2, 2 dc) in same sp as join, *sc in next ch-4 sp, (2 dc, ch 2, 2 dc) in next ch-3 sp; rep from * ending with sc in next ch-4 sp, sl st into top of beg ch-3. Fasten off MC.

Rnd 7 Join CC in center back with a sc, sc in each dc and sc with 2 sc in each ch-2 sp, join with sl st in 1st sc.

Rnds 8–16 Ch 1, sc in same sc as join and in each sc around. Join with sl st in 1st sc. End off CC at end of Rnd 16.

Rnd 17 Join MC with sc at the center underarm on RS, *ch 3, sk 2 sc, sc in next sc, ch 4, sk 3 sc, sc in next sc; rep from * around, end with sl st in 1st sc. 33 (37, 41, 45, 49, 53) shells.

Note: Use a stitch marker to indicate the shell at the center of each underarm. If the number of shells between increases is even, place marker in the shell forward of the armhole. Move markers up as each row is stitched.

Rnd 18 Ch 4, *2 dc in next ch-2 sp, ch 1, 2 dc in next sc, ch 1; rep from * across, ending with dc in last sc, join with sl st in 3rd ch of beg ch-4.

Rnd 19 Sc in next ch-1 sp, *ch 3, sc in next ch-1 sp, ch 4, sc in next ch-1 sp; rep from * around, ending with sl st in beg sc.

Rnd 20 Sl st in next ch-3 sp, ch 3, (dc, ch 2, 2 dc) in same sp as join, *sc in next ch-4 sp, (2 dc, ch 2, 2 dc) in next ch-3 sp; rep from * ending with sc in next ch-4 sp, sl st into top of beg ch-3.

Rnd 21 (38, 41, 44, 47, 50) Ch 4, (*2dc in next ch-2 sp, ch 1, 2dc in next sc, ch 1; rep from * across to sc before next marked shell, 2 dc in dc before next sc, ch 1, 2 dc in sc, ch 1, 2 dc in dc after sc, ch 1, 2 dc in marked shell, ch 1, 2 dc in dc before next sc, ch 1, 2 dc in sc, ch 1, 2 dc after sc; rep from { once more, ending with dc in last sc, join with sl st in 3rd ch of beg ch-4. 37 (41, 45, 49, 53, 57) shells.

Rnd 22–23 Rep Rnds 19–20.

Rnd 24 Rep Rnd 18.

Rnds 25–36 Rep Rnds 22–24 4 times.

Rnd 37 Rep Rnd 21. 41 (45, 49, 53, 57, 61) shells.

Rnds 38–49 Rep Rnds 22–24 4 times.

Rnd 50 Rep Rnd 21. 45 (49, 53, 57, 61, 65) shells.

Rnds 51–62 Rep Rnds 22–24 4 times.

Sizes L (XL, 2X, 3X) only:
Go to Rnd 76.

Sizes 4X and 5X only:

Rnd 63 Rep Rnd 21. 65 (69) shells.

Rnd 64–75 Rep Rnds 22–24 4 times.

All Sizes:

Rnd 76 Rep Rnd 21. 49 (54, 57, 61, 69, 73) shells.

Rnds 77–79 Rep Rnds 22–24.

Rnd 80 Sl st in next dc and ch-2 sp, ch 4, [(dc, ch1) 6 times, dc] in same ch-2 sp, sc in next sc, *[dc, (ch 1, dc) 6 times] in next ch-2 sp, sc in next sc; rep from * around, join with sl st in 3rd ch of beg ch-3. End off.

Sleeve (Make 2)

Rnd 1 With MC, join in sc at underarm, shell in next ch-2 sp, sc in next ch-2 sp, *shell in next ch-3 sp, sc in next ch-4 sp; rep from * around to last 2 ch-2 sps, sc in next ch-2 sp, shell in next ch-2 sp. Join with sl st in beg sc.

Rnd 2 Ch 4, *2 dc in next ch-2 sp, ch 1, 2 dc in next sc, ch 1; rep from * across, ending with dc in last sc, join with sl st in 3rd ch of beg ch-4.

Rnd 3 Sc in next ch-1 sp, *ch 3, sc in next ch-1 sp, ch 4, sc in next ch-1 sp; rep from * around ending with sl st in beg sc.

Rnd 4 Sl st in next ch-3 sp, ch 3, (dc, ch 2, 2 dc) in same sp as join, *sc in next ch-4 sp, (2 dc, ch 2, 2 dc) in next ch-3 sp; rep from * ending with sc in next ch-4 sp, sl st into top of beg ch-3.

Rnds 5–28 Rep Rnds 2–4 8 times more. End off MC at end of Rnd 28.

Rnd 29 Join CC with sc in same ch as join, sc in each dc and sc around, placing 2 dc in each ch-2 sp, join with sl st in 1st sc.

Rnd 30 Ch 1, sc in each sc around; join with sl st in 1st sc.

Rnd 31 Ch 1, sc in same sc as join, *ch 3, sl st in 3rd ch from hook, sk 2 sc, sc in next sc; rep from * around, ending with sl st in 1st sc. End off.

Neck Edging

Rnd 1 Join MC with sc in center back of neck, work 26 (33, 40, 47, 54, 61) sc evenly spaced to corner, sc3tog at inside corner, work 14 (21, 28, 35, 42, 49) sc evenly spaced across from front neck edge to outside corner, 3 sc in corner, work 35 (38, 41, 44, 47, 51) sc evenly spaced along left side of V-neckline, sc3tog at base of V, work 35 (38, 41, 44, 47, 51) sc evenly spaced along right side of V-neckline, 3 sc in corner, work 14 (21, 28, 35, 42, 47) sc evenly spaced across from front neck edge to inside corner, sc3tog at inside corner, work 22 (29, 36, 43, 50, 57) sc evenly spaced across to middle back, join with sl st in 1st sc.

Rnd 2 Ch 1, *sc in each sc to 1 sc before next sc3tog, sc3tog, sc in each sc across to middle sc in next corner, 3 sc in middle sc; rep from * once, sc in each sc to 1 sc before next sc3tog, sc3tog, sc in each sc to end, join with sl st to 1st sc.

Rnd 3 Ch 1, sc in each sc to 1 sc before next sc3tog, sc3tog, sc in each sc across to middle sc in next corner, 3 sc in middle sc, sc in each sc to 1 sc before next sc3tog, sc3tog, sc to 3 sc before middle sc in next corner, ch 5, sc in corner, sc in each sc to 1 sc before next sc3tog, sc3tog, sc in each sc to end, join with sl st to 1st sc. End off.

Weave in all ends.

Sew button onto top of neck in st on left side, opposite buttonhole.

Aperture Tunic Schematic

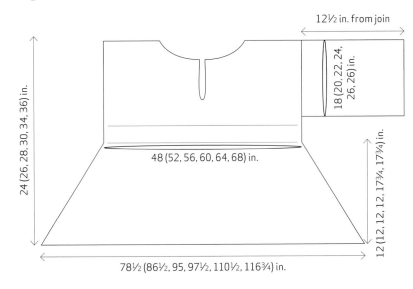

78½ (86½, 95, 97½, 110½, 116¾) in.

48 (52, 56, 60, 64, 68) in.

24 (26, 28, 30, 34, 36) in.

12 (12, 12, 12, 17¾, 17¾) in.

18 (20, 22, 24, 26, 26) in.

12½ in. from join

Aperture Tunic Stitch Diagram

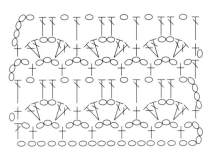

Sweetheart Tank Top

This lightweight top with an out-of-the-ordinary neckline is sure to win a place in every new stitcher's heart. The easy A-line shaping and allover stitch pattern create a classically styled top wearable on its own or as part of a layered look. In the spirit of keeping things simple, the front neckline detail is created by splitting the front garment piece just above the armhole shaping line, working the two sides separately, and letting the center edges fall naturally into place.

Tip: For a higher neckline, simply continue to work the front as one piece, making sure to incorporate all of the armhole shaping until your desired height, then split it. Since there are no neck edge decreases, you can begin the split anywhere you like without confusion.

SKILL LEVEL
Easy

FINISHED BUST
L (XL, 2X, 3X, 4X, 5X); 44 (48, 52, 56, 60, 64) in.

YARN
Red Heart Sport; 4 (4, 4, 5, 6, 6) skeins Black, #12 (70 g/ 165 yds); 1,020 (1,020, 1,122, 1,224, 1,428, 1,530) yds DK weight yarn (CYCA 3 Light, see p. 146)

NOTIONS
Hook size H/8 U.S. (5 mm) *or size needed to obtain gauge*
Stitch marker
Tapestry needle

GAUGE
6 shells and 14 rows = 4 in. in patt st

Back

Loosely ch 122 (128, 134, 146, 152, 164).
Row 1 (Sc, ch 2, sc) in 2nd ch from hook, *sk 2 ch, (sc,ch 2, sc) in next ch. Rep from * to end. Ch 1, turn. 41 (43, 45, 49, 51, 55) shells.
Row 2 (Sc, ch 2, sc) in 1st ch-2 sp, *(sc, ch 2, sc) in next ch-2 sp. Rep from * to end. Ch 1, turn.
Rep Row 2 for pattern until work measures 1 in. from beg.

FIRST DECREASE

Row 1 Sc in 1st ch-2 sp, *(sc, ch 2, sc) in next ch-2 sp. Rep from * across until 1 ch-2 sp remains, sc in last ch-2 sp. Ch 1, turn. 39 (41, 43, 47, 49, 53) shells plus 2 sc.
Row 2 Sc in 1st sc, *(sc, ch 2, sc) in next ch-2 sp. Rep from * to end, sc in last sc. Ch 1, turn.
Rep Row 2 for pattern until work measures 3 in. from beg.

SECOND DECREASE

Row 1 Sl st in 1st sc, *(sc, ch 2, sc) in next ch-2 sp. Rep from * to end, leaving last sc unworked. Ch 1, turn. 39 (41, 43, 47, 49, 53) shells.
Row 2 Rep Row 2 of First Decrease.
Rep Row 2 for pattern until work measures 5 in. from beg.

continued on page 52

Rep First Decrease section until work measures 7 in. from beg. 37 (39, 41, 45, 47, 51) shells plus 2 sc.

Rep Second Decrease section until work measures 9 in. from beg. 37 (39, 41, 45, 47, 51) shells.

Rep First Decrease section until work measures 11 in. from beg. 35 (37, 39, 43, 45, 49) shells plus 2 sc.

Rep Second Decrease section until work measures 12 (12, 13, 13, 14, 14) in. from beg. 35 (37, 39, 43, 45, 49) shells.

ARMHOLE SHAPING

Row 1 Sl st in 1st ch-2 sp, (ch 2, sc in next ch-2 sp) 1 (1, 1, 1, 2, 3) time(s), *(sc, ch 2, sc) in next ch-2 sp. Rep from * until 2 (2, 2, 2, 3, 4) ch-2 sps remain. Ch 1, turn. 31 (33, 35, 39, 39, 41) shells.

Row 2 (Sc, ch 2, sc) in 1st ch-2 sp, *(sc, ch 2, sc) in next ch-2 sp. Rep from * to end. Ch 1, turn.

Rows 3–18 (Rep Rows 1–2 of First Decrease section, then Rows 1–2 of Second Decrease section) 4 times. 23 (25, 27, 31, 31, 33) shells.

Rep Row 2 for pattern until work measures 9 (9½, 10, 10½, 11, 11½) in. from start of Armhole Shaping.

Shoulder Shaping

FIRST SHOULDER

Row 1 Sl st in 1st ch-2 sp, ch 2, sc in next ch-2 sp, (sc, ch 2, sc) in each of next 3 (3, 4, 5, 5, 5) ch-2 sps. Ch 1, turn.

Row 2 (Sc, ch 2 sc) in 1st ch-2 sp and in each of next 1 (1, 2, 2, 2, 2) ch-2 sps, sc in next ch-2 sp. End off.

SECOND SHOULDER

Row 1 Working in same direction as Row 1 of First Shoulder, sk 13 (15, 15, 17, 17, 19) ch-2 sps, (sc, ch 2, sc) in each of next 3 (3, 4, 5, 5, 5) ch-2 sps, sc in next ch-2 sp, leave last ch-2 sp unworked. Ch 1, turn.

Row 2 Sl st in 1st sc, ch 2, sc in next ch-2 sp, (sc, ch 2, sc) in each ch-2 sp to end. End off.

Front

Rep instructions for Back until Row 6 of Armhole Shaping is completed.

Place stitch marker on center ch-2 sp for reference.

NECKLINE SHAPING
LEFT SIDE

Row 1 Sc in 1st ch-2 sp, *(sc, ch 2, sc) in next ch-2 sp. Rep from * to marker, leave marked ch-2 sp unworked. Ch 1, turn. 10 (11, 12, 14, 14, 15) shells plus 1 sc.

Row 2 (Sc, ch 2, sc) in 1st ch-2 sp, *(sc, ch 2, sc) in next ch-2 sp. Rep from * to end, sc in last sc. Ch 1, turn.

Row 3 Sl st in 1st sc, *(sc, ch 2, sc) in next ch-2 sp. Rep from * to end. Ch 1, turn. 10 (11, 12, 14, 14, 15) shells.

Row 4 (Sc, ch 2, sc) in 1st ch-2 sp, *(sc, ch 2, sc) in next ch-2 sp. Rep from * to end. Ch 1, turn.

Rep Rows 1–4 2 (2, 2, 3, 3, 3) more times. 8 (9, 10, 11, 11, 12) shells.

Rep Row 4 for pattern until work measures 9 (9½, 10, 10½, 11, 11½) in. from start of Armhole Shaping, ending with a WS row.

Rep instructions for First Shoulder of Back. End off.

RIGHT SIDE

Row 1 Sk marked st, beginning (sc, ch 2, sc) in 1st ch-2 sp, *(sc, ch 2, sc) in next ch-2 sp. Rep from * across until 1 ch-2 sp remains, sc in last ch-2 sp. Ch 1, turn. 11 (13, 14, 15, 15, 16) shells plus 1 sc.

No extra edgings are needed for this quick-to-crochet top. The neat, shaped edges that this stitch pattern creates as you go are edging enough.

Row 2 Sc in 1st sc, *(sc, ch 2, sc) in next ch-2 sp. Rep from * to end. Ch 1, turn.

Row 3 (Sc, ch 2, sc) in 1st ch-2 sp, *(sc, ch 2, sc) in next ch-2 sp. Rep from * to end, leaving last sc unworked. Ch 1, turn. 11 (13, 14, 15, 15, 16) shells.

Row 4 (Sc, ch 2, sc) in 1st ch-2 sp, *(sc, ch 2, sc) in next ch-2 sp. Rep from * to end. Ch 1, turn.

Rep Rows 1–4 0 (2, 2, 2, 2, 2) more times. 11 (11, 12, 13, 13, 14) shells.

Rep Row 4 for pattern until work measures 9 (9½, 10, 10½, 11, 11½) in. from start of Armhole Shaping, ending with a RS row.

Rep instructions for First Shoulder of Back. End off.

Assembly

Block lightly if desired. Stitch Front to Back at shoulders.

Note: Front shoulders are wider than Back shoulders. Line up the stitches at the outside edges and let the unsewn stitches on Front fall back naturally from the center opening.

Stitch Front to Back at side seams.

Weave in all ends.

Sweetheart Tank Top Schematic

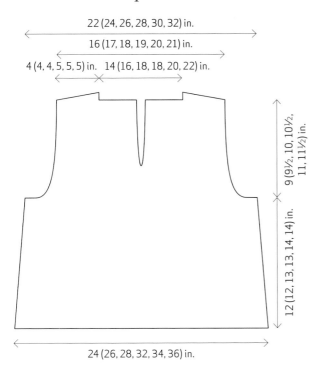

22 (24, 26, 28, 30, 32) in.

16 (17, 18, 19, 20, 21) in.

4 (4, 4, 5, 5, 5) in.   14 (16, 18, 18, 20, 22) in.

9 (9½, 10, 10½, 11, 11½) in.

12 (12, 13, 13, 14, 14) in.

24 (26, 28, 32, 34, 36) in.

Sweetheart Tank Top Stitch Diagram

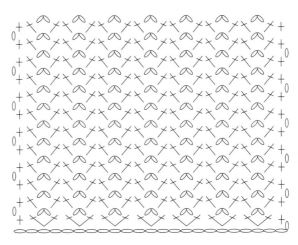

Perfect Base Tank Top

The key to creating perfect layering pieces is to make them in a very fine gauge so they add visual interest without bulk—and without raising your temperature past the point of comfort. And of course the trick to crocheting a project in a very fine gauge *without* dropping over from boredom is to choose an interesting stitch pattern like the one used here.

Tip: If you are a "tucker" rather than a "blouser"—and yes I am talking about hems here—make the tank top longer by adding a few extra inches of stitching, repeating Rows 2 and 3, before shaping the waist.

SKILL LEVEL
Easy

FINISHED BUST
L (XL, 2X, 3X, 4X, 5X); 46 (49, 52, 58, 61, 64) in.

YARN
Kollage Riveting; 4 (4, 5, 5, 6, 6) skeins Night Denim (100 g/350 yds); 1,400 (1,400, 1,750, 1,750, 2,100, 2,100) yds sport weight yarn (CYCA 3, Fine, see p. 146)

NOTIONS
Hook size F/5 U.S. (3.75 mm) *or size needed to obtain gauge*
Tapestry needle

GAUGE
2 shells plus 2 sc and 8 rows = 4 in. in patt st

NOTES
Ch-3 counts as 1 dc throughout.
Shell = (3 dc, ch 1, 3 dc) in specified stitch.

Back
Ch 107 (115, 123, 139, 147, 155).
Row 1 Sc in 2nd ch from hook, *sk 3 ch, shell in next ch, sk 3 ch, sc in next ch. Rep from * to end. Ch 3, turn. 13 (14, 15, 17, 18, 19) shells.
Row 2 3 dc in 1st sc, sc in next ch-1 sp, *shell in next sc, sc in next ch-1 sp. Rep from * to end, 4 dc in last sc. Ch 1, turn. 12 (13, 14, 16, 17, 18) shells plus 2 4-dc shells.
Row 3 Sc in 1st dc, shell in next sc, *sc in next ch-1 sp, shell in next sc. Rep from * to end, sc in last dc. Ch 3, turn. 13 (14, 15, 17, 18, 19) shells.
Rep Rows 2–3 for pattern until work measures 5 in. from beg, ending with a Row 3.

WAIST SHAPING
Row 1 Dc in 1st sc, sc in next ch-1 sp, *shell in next sc, sc in next ch-1 sp. Rep from * to end, 2 dc in last sc. Ch 1, turn. 12 (13, 14, 16, 17, 18) shells plus 2 2-dc shells.
Row 2 Sl st in 1st dc, (2 dc, ch 1, 3 dc) in next sc, sc in next ch-1 sp, *shell in next sc, sc in next ch-1 sp. Rep from * to end, (3 dc, ch 1, 2 dc) in last sc. Ch 1, turn. 11 (12, 13, 15, 16, 17) shells plus 2 partial shells.
Row 3 Sk 1st dc, sl st in next dc, ch 1, sc in ch-1 sp, * shell in next sc, sc in next ch-1 sp. Rep from * to end. Ch 3, turn. 12 (13, 14, 16, 17, 18) shells.
Rows 4–5 Rep Rows 2–3 of Back.
Row 6 (Dc, ch 1, 3 dc) in 1st sc, sc in next ch-1 sp, *shell in next sc, sc in next ch-1 sp. Rep from * to end, (3 dc,

continued on page 56

ch 1, 2 dc) in last sc. Ch 4, turn. 11 (12, 13, 15, 16, 17) shells plus 2 partial shells.

Row 7 3 dc in 4th ch from hook, sc in next ch-1 sp, *shell in next sc, sc in next ch-1 sp. Rep from * to end, 4 dc in last dc. Ch 1, turn. 12 (13, 14, 16, 17, 18) shells plus 2 4-dc shells.

Row 8 Rep Row 3 of Back.

Rep Rows 2–3 of Back for pattern until work measures 14½ (15, 15½, 16, 16½, 17) in. from beg, ending with a Row 3, ch 1, turn after the final Row 3.

ARMHOLE SHAPING

Row 1 Sl st in sc and in each of 3 dc, ch 1, sc in ch-1 sp, *shell in next sc, sc in next ch-1 sp. Rep from * to end. Ch 3, turn. 12 (13, 14, 16, 17, 18) shells.

This top is a perfect example of how even a little bit of waist shaping can accentuate your curves while eliminating extra fabric around the waist, which none of us—no matter our size—wants in a garment.

Row 2–10 Rep Rows 1–3 of Waist Shaping 3 times. 9 (10, 11, 13, 14, 15) shells.

Work even on these sts by repeating Rows 2–3 of Back until work measures 8½ (9, 9½, 10, 10½, 11) in. from start of Armhole Shaping, ending with a Row 3. Ch 1, turn at end of the final Row 3.

RIGHT SHOULDER

Row 1 Sl st in sc and each of 1st 3 dc, ch 1, sc in ch-1 sp, (shell in next sc, sc in next ch-1 sp) 2 (2, 2, 3, 3, 3) times. Ch 2, turn.

Row 2 2 hdc in 1st sc, sc in next ch-1 sp, 5 hdc in next sc, sc in next ch-1 sp. End off.

LEFT SHOULDER

Working from the outer edge toward center, rep instructions for Right Shoulder.

Front

Work as for Back until Row 7 of Armhole Shaping is complete.

NECKLINE SHAPING
LEFT FRONT

Row 1 Dc in 1st sc, sc in next ch-1 sp, (shell in next sc, sc in next ch-1 sp) 3 times, 2 dc in next sc. Ch 1, turn.

Row 2 Sl st in 1st dc, (2 dc, ch 1, 3 dc) in next ch-1 sp, sc in next ch-1 sp, (shell in next sc, sc in next ch-1 sp) 2 times, (3 dc, ch 1, 2 dc) in next sc. Ch 1, turn.

Row 3 Sk 1st dc, sl st in next dc, ch 1, sc in ch-1 sp, *shell in next sc, sc in next ch-1 sp. Rep from * to end. Ch 3, turn.

Row 4 Dc in 1st sc, sc in next ch-1 sp, (shell in next sc, sc in next ch-1 sp) 2 times, 4 dc in next sc. Ch 1, turn.

Row 5 Sc in 1st dc, (shell in next sc, sc in next ch-1 sp) 2 times, (3 dc, ch 1, 2 dc) in next sc. Ch 1, turn.

Row 6 Sk 1st dc, sl st in next dc, ch 1, sc in ch-1 sp, (shell in next sc, sc in next ch-1 sp) 2 times, 4 dc in last sc. Ch 1, turn.

Row 7 Sc in 1st dc, (shell in next sc, sc in next ch-1 sp) 2 times, 2 dc in next sc. Ch 1, turn.

Row 8 Sl st in 1st dc, (2 dc, ch 1, 3 dc) in next sc, sc in next ch-1 sp, shell in next sc, sc in next ch-1 sp, 4 dc in last sc. Ch 1, turn.

Row 9 Sc in 1st dc, (shell in next sc, sc in next ch-1 sp) 2 times. Ch 3, turn.

Row 10 3 dc in 1st sc, sc in next ch-1 sp, shell in next sc, sc in next ch-1 sp, 4 dc in last sc. Ch 1, turn.

Row 11 Sc in 1st dc, shell in next sc, sc in next ch-1 sp, shell in next sc, sc in last dc. Ch 3, turn.

Rep Rows 10–11 for pattern until armhole measures same as Back, ending with a Row 11.

LEFT SHOULDER
Row 1 3 dc in 1st sc, sc in ch-1 sp, shell in next sc, sc in next ch-1 sp. Ch 1, turn.
Row 2 Sl st in each of 1st 3 dc, sc in ch-1 sp, 5 hdc in next sc, sl st in last dc. End off.

RIGHT FRONT
Row 1 Working from outer edge toward center, 2 dc in 1st sc, sc in next ch-1 sp, (shell in next sc, sc in next ch-1 sp) 3 times, 2 dc in next sc. Ch 1, turn.
Rep instructions for Left Front, beginning with Row 2.

Assembly
Block each piece if desired.
Stitch the Front to the Back at the shoulder and side seams.

Bottom Edging
Attach yarn on the opposite side of the foundation ch of the Back by working 1 sc in same ch as sc. Stitch all the way around the bottom edge, placing a shell opposite each shell and a sc opposite each sc. Join rnd with sl st. End off.

Neckline and Armhole Edgings
Rnd 1 Work sc, evenly spaced, all the way around the neckline and armholes. Join rnds with sl st.
Rnds 2–3 Ch 1, sc in each sc around. End off after Rnd 3. Weave in all ends.

Perfect Base Top Tank Schematic

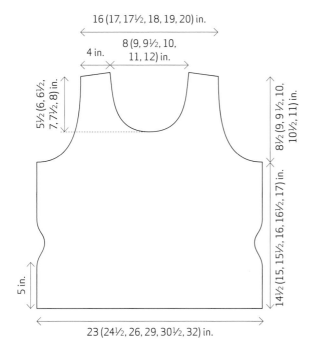

16 (17, 17½, 18, 19, 20) in.

8 (9, 9½, 10, 11, 12) in.

4 in.

5½ (6, 6½, 7, 7½, 8) in.

8½ (9, 9½, 10, 10½, 11) in.

14½ (15, 15½, 16, 16½, 17) in.

5 in.

23 (24½, 26, 29, 30½, 32) in.

Perfect Base Tank Top Stitch Diagram

Orange Marmalade Shell

Classic details make a garment look sophisticated, even if it is easy to stitch. Orange Marmalade has a subtle draped neckline, cropped batwing sleeves, and a ribbed waist embellished with buttons. Choose an alpaca blend yarn instead of pure alpaca to add a soft look with a lot of halo—without making the sweater so warm you can only wear it in sub-zero temperatures! **DESIGNED BY MARLY BIRD**

Tip: If a narrow waist is your best feature, shorten the front and back to get that ribbing right on your waist instead of below it.

SKILL LEVEL
Easy

FINISHED BUST
L (XL, 2X, 3X, 4X, 5X); 46 (50, 54, 58, 62, 66) in.

YARN
Premier™ Yarns Alpaca Dance; 4 (4, 4, 5, 5, 6) skeins Foxy, #03 (100 g/371 yds per skein); 1,484 (1,484, 1,484, 1,855, 1,855, 2,226) yds worsted weight yarn (CYCA 4, Medium, see p. 146)

NOTIONS
Hook size G/6 U.S. (4 mm) *or size needed to obtain gauge*
4 buttons, ⅝ in. or ¾ in. in diameter
Tapestry needle

GAUGE
24 sts and 11 rows = 4 in. in patt st; 20 sts = 4 in. in ribbing patt

Back

Ch 120 (132, 144, 156, 168, 180).

Set-Up Row Sc in 8th ch from hook and next 2 ch, *ch 5, sk 3 ch, sc in next 3 ch; rep from * to last 2 ch, ch 2, sk 1 ch, dc in last ch, turn. 19 (21, 23, 25, 27, 29) pattern repeats.

Row 1 (RS) Ch 1, sc in 1st st, ch 3, sk 1 sc, sc in next sc, *ch 3, sk 1 sc, sc in ch-5 sp, ch 3, sk 1 sc, sc in next sc; rep from * to t-ch, ch 3, sk 1 sc, sc in 3rd ch of t-ch. Ch 1, turn.

Row 2 Sc in 1st sc, sc in ch-3 sp, ch 5, sk 1 sc, sc in next ch-3 sp, sc in sc, *sc in next ch-3 sp, ch 5, sk 1 sc, sc in next ch-3 sp, sc in sc; rep from * to end. Ch 6, turn.

Row 3 Sc into 1st sc, *ch 3, sk 1 sc, sc in ch-5 sp, ch 3, sk 1 sc, sc in next sc; rep from * to end, ch 3, dc into same sc as last sc. Ch 1, turn.

Row 4 Sc into dc, sc into 1st ch-3 sp, *ch 5, sk 1 sc, sc in next ch-3 sp, sc in sc, sc in next ch-3 sp; rep from * to last sc, ch 5, sk 1 sc, sc in ch-6 t-ch, sc in 4th ch of t-ch. Ch 1, turn.

Row 5 Sc in 1st sc, *ch 3, sk 1 sc, sc in ch-5 sp, ch 3, sk 1 sc, sc in next sc; rep from * to end. Ch 6, turn.

Row 6 Sk 1 sc, sc in ch-3 sp, sc in sc, sc in next ch-3 sp, *ch 5, sk 1 sc, sc in next ch-3 sp, sc in sc, sc in next ch-3 sp; rep from * to last sc, ch 2, tr in sc. Ch 1, turn.

Rows 7–24 Rep Rows 1–6. 23 (25, 27, 29, 31, 33) pattern repeats.

Row 25 Rep Row 1.

continued on page 60

Row 26 Rep Row 2.
Row 27 Rep Row 5.
Row 28 Rep Row 6.
Rep Rows 25–28 until work measures 21 (21, 22, 22, 23, 23) in. End off.

Front
Work as for Back to Row 26.
Row 27 Rep Back Row 3.
Row 28 Rep Back Row 4.
Rows 29–38 (29–38, 29–40, 29–40, 29–42, 29–42) Rep Rows 27–28. 35 (37, 41, 43, 47, 49) pattern repeats.
Next 2 Rows Rep Back Rows 5–6.
Continue to rep Back Rows 25–28 until work measures 21 (21, 22, 22, 23, 23) in. End off.

Ribbing
Ch 30.
Set-Up Row Sc in 2nd ch from hook and in each ch across. Ch 1, turn. 29 sts.

Row 1 (WS) Sc in each sc across. Ch 2, turn.
Row 2 (RS) Dc in each sc across. Ch 1, turn.
Row 3 Sc in each dc across. Ch 1, turn.
Row 4 Sc in each sc across. Ch 1, turn.
Rep Rows 1–4 until work measures 38 (42, 46, 50, 54, 58) in.

Assembly
Block pieces to measurements.
Seam shoulders together matching up the armhole edges and leaving an 8-in. opening across the back neck. The extra front neck fabric will drape like a cowl.
Seam sides, leaving armholes open 9 (9, 9½, 9½, 9¾, 9¾) in.
Sew one selvage edge of ribbing evenly along lower edge of body. Seam the Set-Up Row with the last row of the ribbing, then add 4 decorative buttons, evenly spaced along the seam.

Neck and Armhole Trim
Sc 1 rnd evenly around neck and each armhole.

Buttons don't have to be practical. These decorative buttons look great, but don't actually hold anything together. Just stitch them on top of the finished sweater for an extra-special detail.

Orange Marmalade Shell Stitch Diagram

Orange Marmalade Shell Schematics

BACK

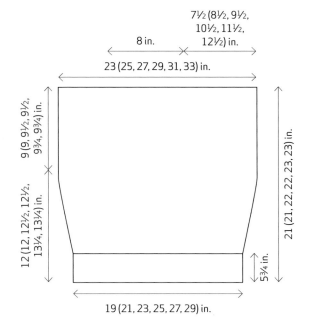

7½ (8½, 9½, 10½, 11½, 12½) in.

8 in.

23 (25, 27, 29, 31, 33) in.

9 (9, 9½, 9½, 9¾, 9¾) in.

12 (12, 12½, 12½, 13¼, 13¼) in.

21 (21, 22, 22, 23, 23) in.

5¾ in.

19 (21, 23, 25, 27, 29) in.

FRONT

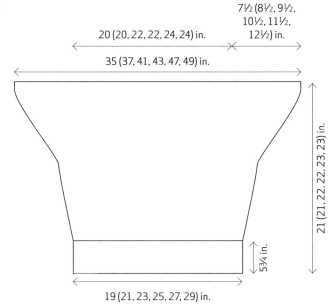

7½ (8½, 9½, 10½, 11½, 12½) in.

20 (20, 22, 22, 24, 24) in.

35 (37, 41, 43, 47, 49) in.

21 (21, 22, 22, 23, 23) in.

5¾ in.

19 (21, 23, 25, 27, 29) in.

CHAPTER
4

Cardigans, Coats, and Jackets

IN THIS CHAPTER, WE WILL TAKE A LOOK AT CARDIGANS AND outerwear. One of the things I love about these types of pieces is that I can be wearing whatever wardrobe basic I own, but look way more put together in a matter of minutes by adding a unique outer layer that suits my individual style.

Try a simple cardigan, such as the Essential Cardigan (p. 64) or the silky Comely Cardigan (p. 76), for the mall or the office, or throw on outerwear such as the Traditional Cloak (p. 96) or Intertwined Poncho (p. 86) to run errands or do the after-school pickup.

Of course, you can customize the fit on these garments to suit your size, but also take into consideration the different looks you can achieve by changing the texture and color of the yarn or the embellishments and closures. These items offer a great chance to use all of those funky handmade buttons or shawl pins you have seen at the yarn shops but didn't have a use for!

Essential Cardigan

We start this chapter with a simple double crochet cardigan. Like the Essential Pullover, this cardigan's simple stitching allows for easy pattern modification, so getting the perfect fit is attainable even for beginners. And, because the pattern stitch is plain in this sweater, you can go crazy with whatever fancy yarn you like—there are no textured stitches fighting for visual supremacy with a multihued or heavily haloed yarn.

Tip: The pieces of the Essential Cardigan are interchangeable with the pieces of the Essential Pullover (p. 20). If you want a shorter length sleeve, you can use the Essential Pullover sleeve schematic.

SKILL LEVEL
Easy

FINISHED BUST
L (XL, 2X, 3X, 4X, 5X); 46 (50, 54, 60, 64, 68) in.

YARN
Berroco Vintage DK; 5 (6, 6, 7, 8, 9) skeins Chana Dal, #2192 (100 g/288 yds); 1,440 (1,728, 1,728, 2,016, 2,304, 2,592) yds DK weight yarn (CYCA 3, Light, see p. 146)

NOTIONS
Hook size G/6 U.S. (4 mm) *or size needed to obtain gauge*
Tapestry needle
5 buttons, ¾ in. in diameter

GAUGE
14 sts and 8 rows = 4 in. in dc

NOTES
Ch-3 counts as 1 dc throughout.
Carefully read the Fronts shaping instructions. For most sizes, neckline and armhole decreases happen together.

Back

Ch 82 (89, 96, 105, 114, 121).
Row 1 (WS) Dc in 4th ch from hook and in each ch across. Ch 3, turn. 80 (87, 94, 103, 112, 119) dc.
(Ch-3 counts as 1 dc here and throughout.)
Row 2 (RS) Dc in each dc across. Ch 3, turn.
Rep Row 2 for pattern until 8 (8, 8, 10, 10, 10) rows have been completed.

WAIST SHAPING

Row 1 Dc2tog, dc in each dc across to last 2 sts, dc2tog. Ch 3, turn. 78 (85, 92, 101, 110, 117).
Rows 2–3 Rep Row 1. 74 (81, 88, 97, 106, 113) dc after Row 3.
Row 4 Dc in each dc across. Ch 3, turn.
Row 5 2 dc in 1st dc, dc in each dc across to last st, 2 dc in last dc. Ch 3, turn. 76 (83, 90, 99, 108, 115) dc.
Rows 6–7 Rep Row 5. 80 (87, 94, 103, 112, 119) dc after Row 7.
Work even on these sts (dc in each dc across) until work measures 15½ (15½, 16, 17, 17½, 17½) in. from beg, ending with a RS row, ch 1, turn after last row.

ARMHOLE SHAPING

Row 1 Sl st in each of 1st 7 (8, 9, 10, 10, 10) dc, ch 3 (counts as 1 dc), dc in each dc across until 6 (7, 8, 9, 9, 9) dc remain. Ch 3, turn. 68 (73, 78, 85, 94, 101) dc.

continued on page 66

Row 2 Dc2tog, dc in each dc across to last 2 sts, dc2tog. Ch 3, turn. 66 (71, 76, 83, 92, 99) dc.
Rows 3–5 Rep Row 2. 60 (65, 70, 77, 86, 93) dc.
Row 6 Dc in each dc across. Ch 3, turn.
Row 7 Rep Row 2. 58 (63, 68, 75, 84, 91) dc.
Rep Rows 6–7 0 (1, 2, 2, 3, 3) time(s). 58 (61, 64, 71, 78, 85) dc.

Sizes L (XL, 2X) only:
Work even until work measures 9 (9½, 10) in. from start of the armhole shaping, ending with a RS row.

Sizes 3X (4X, 5X) only:
Rep Rows 6–7 2 (3, 5) more times. 67 (72, 75) dc.
Work even until work measures 10½ (11, 11½) in. from start of the armhole shaping, ending with a RS row.

Shoulder Shaping (All Sizes)

LEFT SHOULDER
Row 1 Dc in each of the 1st 20 (20, 21, 22, 23, 24) sts. Ch 3, turn.
Row 2 Dc in each of the 1st 5 (5, 6, 6, 6, 7) dc, hdc in each of next 5 (5, 5, 6, 6, 6) dc, sc in each of next 5 (5, 5, 5, 6, 6) dc, end off, leaving remaining 5 (all sizes) dc unworked.

RIGHT SHOULDER
Working in the same direction as Row 1 of Left Shoulder, sk 18 (21, 22, 23, 26, 27) dc, attach yarn in next dc, ch 3, dc in each dc to end. Ch 1, turn. 20 (20, 21, 22, 23, 24) dc.
Row 2 Sl st in each of the 1st 5 dc, sc in each of the next 5 (5, 5, 5, 6, 6) dc, hdc in each of the next 5 (5, 5, 6, 6, 6) dc, dc in each dc to end. End off.

Fronts

RIGHT FRONT
Ch 42 (45, 59, 52, 58, 61).
Row 1 (WS) Dc in 4th ch from hook and in each ch across. Ch 3, turn. 40 (43, 47, 50, 56, 59) dc.
Row 2 (RS) Dc in each dc across. Ch 3, turn.
Rep Row 2 for pattern until 8 (8, 8, 10, 10, 10) rows have been completed.

WAIST SHAPING
Row 1 Dc2tog, dc in each dc across. Ch 3, turn. 39 (42, 46, 49, 55, 58) dc.
Row 2 Dc in each dc across to last 2 sts, dc2tog. Ch 3,

turn. 38 (41, 45, 48, 54, 57) dc.
Row 3 Rep Row 1. 37 (40, 44, 47, 53, 56) dc.
Row 4 Dc in each dc across. Ch 3, turn.
Row 5 2 dc in 1st dc, dc in each dc across. Ch 3, turn. 38 (41, 45, 48, 54, 57) dc.
Row 6 Dc in each dc across to last st, 2 dc in last dc. Ch 3, turn. 39 (42, 46, 49, 55, 58) dc.
Row 7 Rep Row 5. 40 (43, 47, 50, 56, 59) dc.
Work even on these sts until work measures 15½ (15½, 16, 17, 17½, 17½) in. from beg, ending with a RS row, ch 1, turn after last row.

ARMHOLE SHAPING
Row 1 Sl st in each of 1st 7 (8, 9, 10, 10, 10) dc, ch 3 (counts as 1 dc), dc in each dc across. Ch 3, turn. 34 (36, 39, 41, 47, 50) dc.
Row 2 Dc in each dc across to last 2 sts, dc2tog. Ch 3, turn. 33 (35, 38, 40, 46, 49) dc.
Row 3 Dc2tog, dc in each dc across. Ch 3, turn. 32 (34, 37, 39, 45, 48) dc.
Rows 4–5 Rep Rows 2–3. 30 (32, 35, 37, 43, 46) dc after Row 5.
Row 6 Dc in each dc across. Ch 3, turn.
Row 7 Rep Row 3.
Rep Rows 6–7 0 (1, 2, 2, 3, 3) time(s). 30 (30, 31, 33, 37, 40) dc.

Sizes L (XL, 2X) only:
There are no further armhole decreases; continue neckline shaping as established.

Sizes 3X (4X, 5X):
Rep Rows 6–7 2 (3, 5) more times. 29 (31, 30) dc.
There are no further armhole decreases; continue neckline shaping as established.
At the same time when work measures 2 in. from the start of the armhole, begin Neck Edge Shaping.

NECK EDGE SHAPING
While continuing with armhole shaping as written, decrease 1 st at neck edge every row until 20 (20, 21, 22, 23, 24) sts remain.
Work even until front armhole measures same as for back, ending with a RS row. Ch 1, turn after last row.

Shoulder Shaping
Rep Row 2 of Right Shoulder of Back.

LEFT FRONT
Rep instructions for Right Front up to but not including Waist Shaping.

Row 1 Dc in each dc across to last 2 sts, dc2tog. Ch 3, turn. 39 (42, 46, 49, 55, 58) dc.

Row 2 Dc2tog, dc in each dc across. Ch 3, turn. 38 (41, 45, 48, 54, 57) dc.

Row 3 Rep Row 1. 37 (40, 44, 47, 53, 56) dc.

Row 4 Dc in each dc across. Ch 3, turn.

Row 5 Dc in each dc across to last st, 2 dc in last dc. Ch 3, turn. 38 (41, 45, 48, 54, 57) dc.

Row 6 2 dc in 1st dc, dc in each dc across. Ch 3, turn. 39 (42, 46, 49, 55, 58) dc.

Row 7 Rep Row 5. 40 (43, 47, 50, 56, 59) dc.

Work even on these sts until work measures 15½ (15½, 16, 17, 17½, 17½) in. from beg, ending with a RS row, ch 3, turn after the last row.

ARMHOLE SHAPING

Row 1 Dc in each dc across until 6 (7, 8, 9, 9, 9) dc remain unworked. Ch 3, turn. 34 (36, 39, 41, 47, 50) dc.

Row 2 Dc2tog, dc in each dc across. Ch 3, turn. 33 (35, 38, 40, 46, 49) dc.

Row 3 Dc in each dc across to last 2 sts, dc2tog. Ch 3, turn. 32 (34, 37, 39, 45, 48) dc.

Rows 4–5 Rep Rows 2–3. 30 (32, 35, 37, 43, 46) dc after Row 5.

Row 6 Dc in each dc across. Ch 3, turn.

Row 7 Rep Row 3.

Rep Rows 6–7 0 (1, 2, 2, 3, 3, 3) time(s). 30 (30, 31, 33, 37, 40) dc.

Sizes L (XL, 2X) only:

There are no further armhole decreases; continue neckline shaping as established.

Sizes 3X (4X, 5X) only:

Rep Rows 6–7 2 (3, 5) more times. 29 (31, 30) dc. There are no further armhole decreases; continue neckline shaping as established.

At the same time when work measures 2 in. from the start of the armhole, begin Neck Edge Shaping.

NECK EDGE SHAPING

While continuing with armhole shaping as written, decrease 1 st at neck edge every row until 20 (20, 21, 22, 23, 24) sts remain.

Work even until front armhole measures same as for back, ending with a RS row. Ch 1, turn after last row.

Shoulder Shaping

Rep Row 2 of Left Shoulder of Back.

Sleeve (Make 2)

Ch 36 (36, 40, 40, 42, 44).

Row 1 (WS) Dc in 4th ch from hook and in each ch across. 34 (34, 38, 38, 40, 42) dc.

Row 2 2 dc in 1st dc, dc in each dc across to last sc, 2 dc in last dc. 36 (36, 40, 40, 42, 44) dc.

Increase in 1st and last sts (as in Row 2) every WS row 15 (17, 16, 17, 17, 18) times. 64 (68, 70, 72, 74, 78) dc after final increase. Work even if necessary until work measures 16 (16½, 17, 18, 18, 18) in. or desired length to underarm.

SHAPE SLEEVE CAP

Row 1 Sl st in each of 1st 7 (8, 9, 10, 10, 10) dc, ch 3 (counts as 1 dc), dc in each dc across until 6 (7, 8, 9, 9, 9) dc remain. Ch 3, turn. 52 (54, 54, 54, 56, 60) dc.

Row 2 Dc2tog, dc in each dc across to last 2 sts, dc2tog. Ch 3, turn. 50 (52, 52, 52, 54, 58) dc.

Rows 3–5 Rep Row 2. 44 (46, 46, 46, 48, 52) dc.

Row 6 Dc in each dc across. Ch 3, turn.

Row 7 Rep Row 2. 42 (44, 44, 44, 46, 50) dc.

Rep Rows 6–7 0 (1, 2, 2, 3, 3) time(s). 42 (42, 40, 40, 40, 44) dc. Ch 1, turn after the final Row 7.

Next Row Sl st in each of 1st 4 dc, sc, hdc, dc across until 6 sts remain, hdc, sc, sl st in each of last 4 sts. Ch 1, turn. 42 (42, 40, 40, 40, 44) sts, 30 (30, 28, 28, 28, 32) are dcs.

Next Row Sl st in each of 1st 6 sts, sc, hdc, dc across until 8 sts remain, hdc, sc, sl st, turn. 37 (37, 35, 35, 35, 39) sts, 26 (26, 24, 24, 24, 28) are dcs.

Final Row Sl st in each of 1st 6 sts, sc, hdc, dc in each of next 20 (20, 18, 18, 18, 22) dc, hdc, sc, sl st, end off.

Assembly

Block each garment piece.
Stitch Fronts to Back at shoulder seams.
Stitch Sleeves into armhole openings, easing to fit.
Stitch side seam and sleeve seam on each side.

Edgings

SET-UP

Rnd 1 With RS facing, work 1 rnd of sc around assembled garment, starting in any st at the bottom edge of the Back. Work in the opposite side of the foundation ch across the Back, up the Right Front, across the Right neckline, the Back neckline, the Left neckline, and then the Left Front, and across the Back

continued on page 68

One way to dress a simple sweater up or down is to change the buttons or the edgings. Let those quick additions do the fancy work, and keep the stitching simple.

until you come to your first st. Join rnd with sl st in the 1st sc, end off.

BUTTONHOLE BAND

Row 1 With WS facing, sc in each sc along Right Front. Ch 1, turn. Count how many sts you have. This sample had 58 sts.

Now for a little math! For 5 buttonholes as shown, deduct 10 sts from your count, 2 sts for each buttonhole: $58 - 10 = 48$. Divide the remainder by 4: $48 \div 4 = 12$. Now take one less than your product and multiply it by 4: $4 \times 11 = 44$, with 4 left over.

In this example, I will have 2 sc at beg of the band, 5 buttonholes with 11 sts between each, and 2 sc at the end of the band. If your number doesn't divide evenly by 4, you can fudge by adding or subtracting a st at the beg and/or end of the band. You are now ready to continue.

Row 2 Sc in each sc across. Ch 1, turn.

Row 3 Sc in each of 1st 2 sc, (ch 2, sk 2 sc, sc in each of the next 11 sc) 4 times, ch 2, sk 2 sc, sc in each of the last 2 sc. Ch 1, turn.

Row 4 Sc in each sc across, placing 2 sc in each ch-2 sp. Ch 1, turn.

Row 5 Rep Row 2. End off.

BUTTON BAND

Row 1 With WS facing, sc in each sc across Left Front. Ch 1, turn.

Rows 2–5 Sc in each sc across. Ch 1, turn. End off after Row 5.

PICOT EDGING

Rnd 1 Beginning at the center of the bottom hem of the Back, attach yarn with a sl st. *Ch 3, sl st in 2nd ch from hook, sl st in each of the next 2 sc. Rep from * all the way around the garment, join rnd with sl st in 1st st. End off.

Line up the Buttonhole Band over the Button Band and mark the placement of buttons.

Stitch each button into place.

Essential Cardigan Schematics

BACK

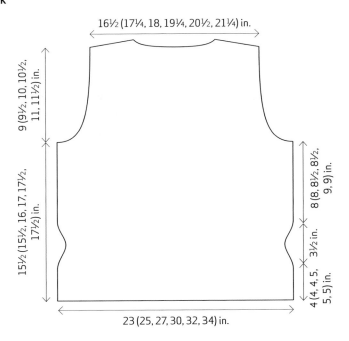

16½ (17¼, 18, 19¼, 20½, 21¼) in.

9 (9½, 10, 10½, 11, 11½) in.

15½ (15½, 16, 17, 17½, 17½) in.

8 (8, 8½, 8½, 9, 9) in.

3½ in.

4 (4, 4, 5, 5, 5) in.

23 (25, 27, 30, 32, 34) in.

FRONT

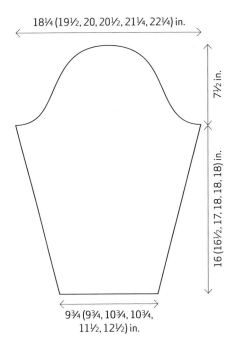

9 (9½, 10, 10½, 11, 11½) in.

7 (7½, 8, 8½, 9, 9½) in.

2 in.

15½ (15½, 16, 17, 17½, 17½) in.

11½ (12½, 13½, 15, 16, 17) in.

SLEEVE

18¼ (19½, 20, 20½, 21¼, 22¼) in.

7½ in.

16 (16½, 17, 18, 18, 18) in.

9¾ (9¾, 10¾, 10¾, 11½, 12½) in.

Dulcet Wrap Cardigan

Wrap sweaters are so comfortable to wear because the fit can be adjusted every time you put them on—a little tighter over a tank top, a little looser over a long-sleeved shirt. Use a lightweight yarn so the wrap doesn't look too thick, and a cotton or cotton blend so it's not too warm to wear indoors.

Tip: You can adjust the fit by tying, and you can add shaping by changing hook size: Use a smaller hook to stitch the lace pattern before the color change (if your waist is smaller than your bust), or after (if your bust is smaller than your waist).

SKILL LEVEL
Intermediate

FINISHED BUST
L (XL, 2X, 3X, 4X, 5X); 43 (47½, 52, 56, 60½, 64½) in. *when tied, can be adjusted when worn.*

YARN
Cascade Ultra Pima; 5 (5, 6, 6, 7, 7) skeins Jade, #3735 (MC), and 2 (2, 2, 2, 3, 3) skeins Teal, #3734 (CC) (100 g/ 220 yds); 1,540 (1,540, 1,760, 1,760, 2,200, 2,200) yds DK weight yarn (CYCA 3, Light, see p. 146)

NOTIONS
Hook size G/6 U.S. (4 mm) *or size needed to obtain gauge*
2 stitch markers

GAUGE
15 sts and 12 rows = 4 in. in patt st

NOTES
Ch-3 counts as 1 dc throughout.
Ch-4 counts as 1 dc plus ch-1 sp throughout.

Ch-5 counts as 1 dc plus ch-2 sp throughout.
Move up stitch markers one row each time you come to them.

Back Set-Up
With CC, loosely ch 83 (91, 99, 107, 115, 123).
Row 1 Dc in 4th ch from hook and in next ch, ch 2, sk 1 ch, sc in next ch, *ch 2, sk 1 ch, dc in each of 5 ch, ch 2, sk 1 ch, sc in next ch. Rep from * to end, ch 2, sk 1 ch, dc in each of 3 ch. Ch 1, turn. 9 (10, 11, 12, 13, 14) 5-dc groups plus 2 3-dc groups.
Row 2 Sc in each of 1st 3 dc, ch 1, dc in next sc, ch 1, *sc in each of next 5 dc, ch 1, dc in next sc, ch 1. Rep from * to end, sc in each of last 3 dc. Ch 1, turn.
Row 3 Sc in 1st sc, *ch 2, sk 1 sc, (dc in next st, dc in ch-1 sp) 2 times, dc in next sc, ch 2, sk 1 sc, sc in next sc. Rep from * to end. Ch 4, turn. 10 (11, 12, 13, 14, 15) 5-dc groups.
Row 4 Sk 1st sc, sc in each of 5 dc, *ch 1, dc in next sc, ch 1, sc in each of 5 dc. Rep from * to end, ch 1, dc in last sc. Ch 3, turn.
Row 5 Dc in ch-1 sp, dc in next sc, ch 2, sk 1 sc, sc in next sc, *ch 2, sk 1 sc, (dc in next st, dc in ch-1 sp) 2 times, dc in next sc, ch 2, sk 1 sc, sc in next sc. Rep from * to end, ch 2, sk 1 sc, dc in next sc, dc in sp created by t-ch, dc in 3rd ch of t-ch. Ch 1, turn.
Rows 6–8 Rep Rows 2–4.
Rows 9–14 Rep Rows 5–8, then Rows 5–6. Do not ch 1 after Row 14.

continued on page 72

Front Set-Up (Make 2)

With CC, ch 67 (75, 83, 91, 99, 107).

Rep Rows 1–14 of Back Set-Up. 8 (9, 10, 11, 12, 13) 5-dc groups. Do not ch 1 after Row 14 of first Front Set-Up, ch 1, turn after Row 14 of second Front Set-Up.

Body

Row 1 (WS) Continuing on 2nd Front Set-Up, sc in 1st sc, *ch 2, sk 1 sc, (dc in next st, dc in ch-1 sp) 2 times, dc in next sc, ch 2, sk 1 sc, sc in next sc. Rep from * 6 (7, 8, 9, 10, 11) times, ch 2, sk 1 sc, (dc in next st, dc in ch-1 sp) 2 times, dc in next sc, ch 2, sc2tog using last sc of Front Set-Up and 1st sc of Back Set-Up, place marker st just completed, **ch 2, sk 1 sc, (dc in next st, dc in ch-1 sp) 2 times, dc in next sc, ch 2, sk 1 sc, sc in next sc. Rep from ** 8 (9, 10, 11, 12, 13) more times, ch 2, sk 1 sc, (dc in next st, dc in ch-1 sp) 2 times, dc in next sc, ch 1, sc2tog using last sc of Back Set-Up and 1st sc of 2nd Front Set-Up, place marker in st just completed, ***ch 2, sk 1 sc, (dc in next st, dc in ch-1 sp) 2 times, dc in next sc, ch 2, sk 1 sc, sc in next sc. Rep from *** to end. Ch 4, turn. 25 (28, 31, 34, 37, 40) 5-dc groups.

Rows 2–14 (14, 14, 18, 18, 18) Rep Row 8 of Back Set-Up, then Rows 5–8 of Back Set-Up 3 (3, 3, 4, 4, 4) times.

Next 2 Rows Change to MC, rep Rows 5–6 of Back Set-Up.

NECKLINE DECREASES

Row 1 (RS) Sc in 1st sc, *ch 2, sk 1 sc, (dc in next st, dc in ch-1 sp) 2 times, dc in next sc, ch 2, sk 1 sc, sc in next sc. Rep from * to end. Ch 1, turn.

Row 2 Sl st in 1st sc and in each of next 2 ch and 2 dc, sc in each of next 3 dc, *ch 1, dc in next sc, ch 1, sc in each of 5 dc. Rep from * until 1 5-dc group remains, ch 1, dc in next sc, ch 1, sc in each of next 3 dc. Ch 1, turn. 24 (27, 31, 33, 36, 39) 5-dc groups.

Rep Rows 1–2 for pattern until work measures 12 (12, 13, 13, 14, 14) in. or desired length to underarm, ending with a Row 2.

Note: The number of 5-dc groups at this point may vary depending on your row gauge. The rest of the pattern is written based on the number of stitches from the markers, so all will be well no matter how many rows it took you to get to this point.

Divide Fronts from Back

RIGHT FRONT

If marker is in a dc: **Row 1 (RS)** Sc in 1st sc, *ch 2, sk 1 sc, (dc in next st, dc in ch-1 sp) 2 times, dc in next sc, ch 2,

sk 1 sc, sc in next sc. Rep from * to 3rd sc before marked st. Ch 1, turn.

If marker is in a sc: **Row 1 (RS)** Sc in 1st sc, *ch 2, sk 1 sc, (dc in next st, dc in ch-1 sp) 2 times, dc in next sc, ch 2, sk 1 sc, sc in next sc. Rep from * to dc before marked st. Ch 1, turn.

Row 2 Rep Row 2 of Neckline Decreases.

Row 3 Rep Row 1 of Neckline Decreases, ch 4, turn.

Row 4 Sk 1st sc, sc in each of 5 dc, *ch 1, dc in next sc, ch 1, sc in each of 5 dc. Rep from * until 1 5-dc group remains, ch 1, dc in next sc, ch 1, sc in each of 3 dc. Ch 1, turn.

Row 5 Sc in 1st sc, *ch 2, sk 1 sc, (dc in next st, dc in ch-1 sp) 2 times, dc in next sc, ch 2, sk 1 sc, sc in next sc. Rep from * to end, ch 2, sk 1 sc, dc in next dc, dc in sp created by t-ch, dc in 3rd ch of t-ch. Ch 1, turn.

Row 6 Sc in each of 1st 3 dc, ch 1, dc in next sc, ch 1, *sc in each of next 5 dc, ch 1, dc in next sc, ch 1. Rep from * to end, sc in each of next 3 dc. Ch 1, turn.

Row 7 Sc in 1st sc, *ch 2, sk 1 sc, (dc in next st, dc in ch-1 sp) 2 times, dc in next sc, ch 2, sk 1 sc, sc in next sc. Rep from * to end. Ch 4, turn.

Rep Rows 4–7 for pattern until 1 5-dc group and 1 3-dc group remains. Work even on these sts until work measures 10 (10, 11¼, 11¼, 12½, 12½) in. from start of Front/Back division, ending with a WS row. Ch 3, turn after the final row.

SHOULDER SHAPING

Working in each st and ch-1 sp across, dc in each of 4 sts, hdc in each of 4 sts, sc in each of 3 sts, sl st to end. End off.

BACK

Continuing in same direction as Right Front, if marker is in a dc: **Row 1** Sk 2 sc, sc in next sc, *ch 2, sk 1 sc, (dc in next st, dc in ch-1 sp) 2 times, dc in next sc, ch 2, sk 1 sc, sc in next sc. Rep from * to 3rd sc before marked st. Ch 1, turn.

Continuing in same direction as Right Front, if marker is in a sc: **Row 1** Sc in 1st dc after marked st, *ch 2, sk 1 sc, (dc in next st, dc in ch-1 sp) 2 times, dc in next sc, ch 2, sk 1 sc, sc in next sc. Rep from * to dc before marked st. Ch 1, turn.

Row 2 Rep Row 2 of Neckline Decreases.

Row 3 Rep Row 1 of Neckline Decreases.

Size L and XL only:

Ch 4, turn, go to Work Even. Sizes 2X (3X, 4X, 5X): Ch 1, turn.

Rows 4–7 (7, 11, 11) Rep Rows 2–3 2 (2, 4, 4) times. Ch 4, turn after the final row.

Work Even

Work even by repeating Rows 5–8 of Back Set-Up, beginning with a Row 8, until work measures 10 (10, 11¼, 11¼, 12½, 12½) in. from start of Front/Back division, ending with a WS row.

LEFT SHOULDER

Working in each st and ch-1 sp across, sl st in each of 1st 2 sts, sc in each of 3 sts, hdc in each of 4 sts, dc in each st to end. End off.

RIGHT SHOULDER

Starting 14 sts in from opposite outside edge, rep Shoulder Shaping from Right Front.

LEFT FRONT

Work in same direction as Row 1 of Right Front.

If marker is in a dc: **Row 1 (RS)** Sk 2 sc after marked st, sc in next sc, *ch 2, sk 1 sc, (dc in next st, dc in ch-1 sp) 2 times, dc in next sc, ch 2, sk 1 sc, sc in next sc. Rep from * end. Ch 1, turn.

If marker is in a sc: **Row 1 (RS)** Sc in 1st dc after marker, *ch 2, sk 1 sc, (dc in next st, dc in ch-1 sp) 2 times, dc in next sc, ch 2, sk 1 sc, sc in next sc. Rep from * to end. Ch 1, turn.

Row 2 Rep Row 2 of Neckline Decreases.

Row 3 Rep Row 1 of Neckline Decreases.

Row 4 Sl st in 1st sc and in each of next 2 ch and 2 dc, sc in each of next 3 dc, *ch 1, dc in next sc, ch 1, sc in each of 5 dc. Rep from * to end, ch 1, dc in next sc. Ch 3, turn.

Row 5 Dc in ch-1 sp, dc in next sc, *ch 2, sk 1 sc, (dc in next st, dc in ch-1 sp) 2 times, dc in next sc, ch 2, sk 1 sc, sc in next sc. Rep from * to end. Ch 1, turn.

Row 6 Sl st in 1st sc and in each of next 2 ch and 2 dc, sc in each of next 3 dc, ch 1, dc in next sc, ch 1, *sc in each of next 5 dc, ch 1, dc in next sc, ch 1. Rep from * to end, sc in each of last 3 dc. Ch 1, turn.

Row 7 Sc in 1st sc, *ch 2, sk 1 sc, (dc in next st, dc in ch-1 sp) 2 times, dc in next sc, ch 2, sk 1 sc, sc in next sc. Rep from * to end. Ch 1, turn.

Rep Rows 4–7 for pattern until 1 5-dc group and 1 3-dc group remain. Work even on these sts until work measures 10 (10, 11¼, 11¼, 12½, 12½) in. from start of Front/Back division, ending with a WS row. Ch 1, turn after the final row.

Big blocks of color add visual interest without adding difficulty to the stitching. Minimize the waist by placing the darker shade on the lower section of the cardigan as I did in the sample, or swap the colors to minimize the bust.

SHOULDER SHAPING

Working in each st and ch-1 sp across, sl st in each of 1st 2 sts, sc in each of 3 sts, hdc in each of 4 sts, dc in each st to end. End off.

Sleeve (Make 2)

With MC, loosely ch 35 (35, 43, 43, 51, 51).

Rows 1–4 Rep Rows 1–4 of Back Set-Up. 4 (4, 5, 5, 6, 6) 5-dc groups.

Row 5 2 dc in 1st dc, dc in ch-1 sp, dc in next sc, ch 2, sk 1 sc, sc in next sc, *ch 2, sk 1 sc, (dc in next st, dc in ch-1 sp) 2 times, dc in next sc, ch 2, sk 1 sc, sc in next sc. Rep from * to end, ch 2, sk 1 sc, dc in next sc, dc in sp created

continued on page 74

by t-ch, 3 dc in 3rd ch of t-ch. Ch 1, turn. 5 (5, 6, 6, 7, 7) 5-dc groups.

Row 6 Sc in each of 1st 5 dc, ch 1, dc in next sc, ch 1, *sc in each of next 5 dc, ch 1, dc in next sc, ch 1. Rep from * to end, sc in each of last 5 sc. Ch 5, turn.

Row 7 Sk 1st 2 sc, sc in next sc, *ch 2, sk 1 sc, (dc in next st, dc in ch-1 sp) 2 times, dc in next sc, ch 2, sk 1 sc, sc in next sc. Rep from * to end, ch 2, sk 1 sc, dc in last sc. Ch 1, turn.

Row 8 Sc in 1st dc, ch 1, dc in next sc, ch 1, *sc in each of next 5 sc, ch 1, dc in next sc, ch 1. Rep from * to end, sc in 3rd ch of t-ch. Ch 3, turn.

Row 9 (Dc in next ch-1 sp, dc in next st) 2 times, *ch 2, sk 1 sc, sc in next sc, ch 2, sk 1 sc, (dc in next st, dc in ch-1 sp) 2 times, dc in next sc. Rep from * to end. Ch 1, turn.

Row 10 Rep Row 6. Ch 3, turn.

Row 11 2 dc in 1st dc, ch 2, sk 1 sc, sc in next sc, *ch 2, sk 1 sc, (dc in next st, dc in ch-1 sp) 2 times, dc in next sc, ch 2, sk 1 sc, sc in next sc. Rep from * to end, ch 2, sk 1 sc, 3 dc in next sc. Ch 1, turn. 4 (4, 5, 5, 6, 6) 5-dc groups plus 2 3-dc groups.

Row 12 Sc in each of 1st 3 dc, ch 1, dc in next sc, ch 1, *sc in each of next 5 sc, ch 1, dc in next sc, ch 1. Rep from * to end, sc in each of last 3 sc. Ch 1, turn.

Row 13 Sc in 1st sc, *ch 2, sk 1 sc, (dc in next st, dc in ch-1 sp) 2 times, dc in next sc, ch 2, sk 1 sc, sc in next sc. Rep from * to end. Ch 4, turn.

Row 14 Sc in each of 1st 5 dc, *ch 1, dc in next sc, ch 1, sc in each of next 5 dc. Rep from * to end, ch 1, dc in last sc. Ch 3, turn.

Rep Rows 5–14 3 (3, 4, 4, 5, 5) times. 8 (8, 10, 10, 12, 12) 5-dc groups.

Work even by repeating Rows 5–8 of Back Set-Up until Sleeve measures 16½ (17, 17, 17½, 18, 18½) in. from beg, ending with a Row 8. Ch 1, turn after the final Row 8.

SHAPE SLEEVE CAP

Row 1 Sl st in 1st dc, sl st in ch-1 sp, sl st in each of next 5 sc, sl st in ch-1 sp, sl st in dc, ch 3, dc in ch-1 sp, dc in next sc, *ch 2, sk 1 sc, sc in next sc, ch 2, sk 1 sc, (dc in next st, dc in ch-1 sp) 2 times, dc in next sc. Rep from * until 6 sts remain, ch 2, sk 1 sc, sc in next sc, ch 2, sk 1 sc, dc in next sc, dc in ch-1 sp, dc in next sc. Ch 1, turn. 5 (5, 7, 7, 9, 9,) 5-dc groups plus 2 3-dc groups.

Row 2 Sc in each of 1st 3 dc, ch 1, dc in next sc, ch 1, *sc in each of next 5 dc, ch 1, dc in next sc, ch 1. Rep from * to end, sc in each of next 3 dc. Ch 1, turn.

Row 3 Sl st in each of 1st 3 sc, sl st in ch-1 sp, sl st in dc, ch 3, dc in ch-1 sp, dc in next sc, *ch 2, sk 1 sc, sc in next sc, ch 2, sk 1 sc, (dc in next st, dc in ch-1 sp) 2 times, dc in next sc. Rep from * until 6 sts remain, ch 2, sk 1 sc, sc in next sc, ch 2, sk 1 sc, dc in next sc, dc in ch-1 sp, dc in next sc. Ch 1, turn. 4 (4, 6, 6, 8, 8) 5-dc groups plus 2 3-dc groups.

Rows 4–6 (6, 8, 8, 8, 8) Rep Rows 2–3 1 (1, 2, 2, 2, 2) times, then Row 2 once more. 3 (3, 4, 4, 6, 6) 5-dc groups plus 2 3-dc groups.

Row 7 (7, 9, 9, 9, 9) Sc in 1st sc, *ch 2, sk 1 sc, (dc in next st, dc in ch-1 sp) 2 times, dc in next sc, ch 2, sk 1 sc, sc in next sc. Rep from * to end. Ch 4, turn.

Row 8 (8, 10, 10, 10, 10) Sk 1st sc, sc in each of 5 dc, *ch 1, dc in next sc, ch 1, sc in each of 5 dc. Rep from * to end, ch 1, dc in last sc. Ch 3, turn.

Row 9 (9, 11, 11, 11, 11) Dc in ch-1 sp, dc in next sc, ch 2, sk 1 sc, sc in next sc, *ch 2, sk 1 sc, (dc in next st, dc in ch-1 sp) 2 times, dc in next sc, ch 2, sk 1 sc, sc in next sc. Rep from * to end, ch 2, sk 1 sc, dc in next sc, dc in sp created by t-ch, dc in 3rd ch of t-ch. Ch 1, turn.

Rows 10 (10, 12, 12, 12, 12)–13 (13, 17, 17, 17, 17) Rep Rows 2–3 2 (2, 3, 3, 3, 3) times, then Row 2 once more. End off. 1 (1, 1, 1, 2, 2) ch-5 groups plus 2 3-dc groups.

Ties (Make 4)

With CC, ch 76 or the desired length of tie, sc in 2nd ch from hook and in each ch across. End off.

Assembly and Edging

Sew Fronts to Back at shoulders.

Sew underarm seam of each Sleeve.

Stitch Sleeves into place in openings.

With CC, sc all the way around the entire garment once, then add a 2nd row of sc across the neckline from point to point.

Tack one tie into place on the outside edge of each Front where the neckline decreases begin. Tack one tie on the inside at the color change where the side seam would be and tack the remaining tie on the outside at the color change where the other side seam would be.

Dulcet Wrap Cardigan Schematics

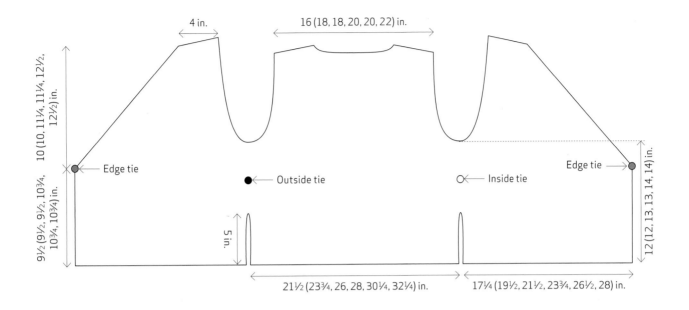

4 in.

16 (18, 18, 20, 20, 22) in.

10 (10, 11¼, 11¼, 12½, 12½) in.

9½ (9½, 9½, 10¾, 10¾, 10¾) in.

Edge tie

● → Outside tie

○← → Inside tie

Edge tie →

12 (12, 13, 13, 14, 14) in.

5 in.

21½ (23¾, 26, 28, 30¼, 32¼) in.

17¼ (19½, 21½, 23¾, 26½, 28) in.

SLEEVE

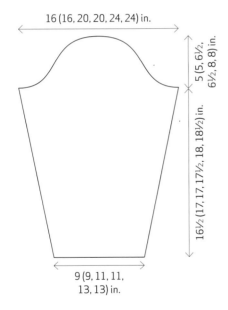

16 (16, 20, 20, 24, 24) in.

5 (5, 6½, 6½, 8, 8) in.

16½ (17, 17, 17½, 18, 18½) in.

9 (9, 11, 11, 13, 13) in.

Comely Cardigan

Ribbing is worked at the bottom of many sweaters for two reasons: to draw the work in so it's closer to the body and to add some vertical lines to what is essentially a horizontal project. Sometimes a sweater pulling in at the hem is a good thing, sometimes a bad thing—it all depends on your individual shape.

Tip: Elasticity is something to take into consideration when selecting a yarn for any project; sometimes you want it and sometimes you don't. By using a single crochet ribbing in a yarn without too much elasticity, you get the strong vertical lines without uncomfortable tightness at the waist.

SKILL LEVEL
Intermediate

FINISHED BUST
L (XL, 2X, 3X, 4X, 5X); 44 (48, 52, 56, 60, 64) in.

YARN
Himalaya Yarns Duke Silk; 7 (7, 8, 9, 11,12) skeins #SI-025 (100 g/225 yds); 1,575 (1,575, 1,800, 2,025, 2,475, 2,700) yds light worsted weight yarn (CYCA 3, Light, see p. 146)

NOTIONS
Hook size H/8 U.S. (5 mm) *or size need to obtain gauge*
2 stitch markers

GAUGE
15 sts and 18 rows = 4 in. in ribbing patt; 14 sts and 10 rows = 4 in. in ldc

NOTE
For linked double crochet (ldc) instructions, see Techniques and Stitches, p. 140.

Ribbing

Ch 16.
Row 1 Sc in 2nd ch from hook and in each ch across. Ch 1, turn. 15 sc.
Row 2 Sctbl across. Ch 1, turn.
Rep Row 2 for pattern until work measures 40 (44, 48, 52, 56, 60) in. End off.

Body

Fold the piece so the two ends meet at the center front for the cardigan opening, place markers on the last row worked where the side seams would be.
Row 1 (RS) Work 40 (44, 48, 52, 56, 60) sc evenly spaced along the top of Ribbing to first marker (right front), 72 (79, 86, 93, 100, 107) sc evenly spaced to 2nd marker (back), 40 (44, 48, 52, 56, 60) sc evenly spaced to end (left front), ch 3, turn. 152 (167, 182, 197, 212, 227) sc. Work even in ldc until work measures 10 (11, 12, 12, 13, 13) in. from beg, ending with a WS row.

RIGHT FRONT
Row 1 Ldc in each of 34 (38, 40, 44, 48, 52) ldc. Ch 3, turn.
Row 2 Ldc2tog, ldc in each ldc across. Ch 3, turn. 33 (37, 39, 43, 47, 51) ldc.
Row 3 Ldc in each ldc to last 2 ldc, ldc2tog. Ch 3, turn. 32 (36, 38, 41, 46, 50) ldc.
Rows 4–5 Rep Rows 2–3. 30 (34, 36, 39, 44, 48) ldc. Size L (XL, 2X) only, no further armhole edge decreases; go to Neck Edge Shaping.

continued on page 78

Sizes 3X (4X, 5X):
Row 6 Rep Row 2. 33 (36, 41) ldc.
Row 7 Ldc in each ldc across. Ch 3, turn.
Row 8 Rep Row 2. 32 (35, 40) ldc.
Rep Rows 7–8 2 (2, 3) times. 30 (33, 37) ldc. No further armhole edge decreases; go to Neck Edge Shaping.
At the same time, when work measures 2 in. from start of armhole, begin Neck Edge Shaping.

Neck Edge Shaping

While continuing with armhole shaping as written, dec 1 st by working a ldc2tog at neck edge every row until 16 (17, 18, 18, 18, 18) ldc remain.

Work even until work measures 9 (9½, 10, 10½, 11, 11½) in. from start of armhole shaping, ending with a WS row.

The smooth face of a fabric of linked stitches, as shown here, offers a terrific canvas for the color variations in multicolored or hand-dyed yarns.

SHOULDER SHAPING
Row 1 Ldc in each of 1st 5 ldc, lhdc in each of next 5 ldc, sc in each of next 4 ldc. End off.

BACK
Working on last row of Body, with RS facing, sk 12 (12, 16, 16, 16, 16) sts from last st of Row 1 of Right Front.
Row 1 Ldc in each of 60 (67, 70, 77, 84, 91) ldc, ch 3, turn. Size L only, go to Work Even.
Row 2 Ldc2tog, ldc in each ldc across to last 2 sts, ldc2tog. Ch 3, turn. 65 (68, 75, 82, 89) ldc.
Rows 3–4 Rep Row 2. 61 (64, 71, 78, 85) ldc. Sizes XL and 2X only, go to Work Even.
Row 5 Rep Row 2. 69 (76, 83) ldc.
Row 6 Ldc in each ldc across. Ch 3, turn.
Row 7 Rep Row 2. 67 (74, 81) ldc.
Rep Rows 6–7 2 (2, 3) times. 63 (70, 75) ldc.

WORK EVEN
Work even (ldc in each ldc across) until work measures 9 (9½, 10, 10½, 11, 11½) in. from start of armhole shaping, ending with a WS row.

SHOULDER SHAPING
RIGHT SHOULDER
Row 1 Ldc in each of 1st 16 (17, 18, 18, 18, 18) ldc. Ch 3, turn.
Row 2 Ldc in each of 1st 5 ldc, lhdc in each of next 5 ldc, sc in each of next 4 ldc. End off.

LEFT SHOULDER
Row 1 Working in the same direction as Row 1 of Right Shoulder, sk 28 (27, 28, 27, 34, 39) ldc, attach yarn with sl st in next ldc, ch 3, ldc in each ldc to end. Ch 1, turn. 16 (17, 18, 18, 18, 18) ldc.
Row 2 Sl st in each of 1st 2 (3, 4, 4, 4, 4) ldc, sc in each of next 4 ldc, lhdc in each of next 5 ldc, ldc in each ldc to end. End off.

LEFT FRONT
Working on last row of Body, with RS facing, sk 12 (12, 16, 16, 16, 16) sts from last st of Row 1 of Right Front.
Row 1 Ldc in each ldc across to end. Ch 3, turn. 34 (38, 40, 44, 48, 52) ldc.
Row 2 Ldc in each ldc across to last 2 sts, ldc2tog. Ch 3, turn. 33 (37, 39, 43, 47, 51) ldc.
Row 3 Ldc2tog, ldc in each ldc across. Ch 3, turn. 32 (36, 38, 41, 46, 50) ldc.
Rows 4–5 Rep Rows 2–3. Sizes L (XL, 2X) only, no further armhole edge decreases; go to Neck Edge Shaping.

Sizes 3X (4X, 5X) only:

Row 6 Rep Row 2. 33 (36, 41) ldc.

Row 7 Ldc in each ldc across. Ch 3, turn.

Row 8 Rep Row 2. 32 (35, 40) ldc.

Rep Rows 7–8 2 (2, 3) times. 30 (33, 37) ldc. No further armhole edge decreases; go to Neck Edge Shaping.

At the same time, when work measures 2 in. from start of armhole, begin Neck Edge Shaping.

Neck Edge Shaping

While continuing with armhole shaping as written, dec 1 st by working an ldc2tog at neck edge every row until 16 (17, 18, 18, 18, 18) ldc remain.

Work even until work measures 9 (9½, 10, 10½, 11, 11½) in. from start of armhole shaping, ending with a WS row.

Sleeve (Make 2)

RIBBING

Ch 9.

Row 1 Sc in 2nd ch from hook and in each ch across. Ch 1, turn. 8 sc.

Row 2 Sc in blo of each sc across. Ch 1, turn.

Rep Row 2 for pattern until work measures 15 (16, 17, 18, 19½, 21) in. End off.

SLEEVE INCREASES

Row 1 With RS facing you, work 56 (60, 63, 68, 74, 79) sc evenly spaced along the long side of Ribbing. Ch 3, turn.

Row 2 2 ldc in 1st sc, ldc in each sc across to last st, 2 ldc in last sc. Ch 3, turn. 58 (62, 65, 70, 76, 81) ldc.

Row 3 Ldc in each ldc across, ch 3, turn.

Row 4 2 ldc in 1st ldc, ldc in each ldc across to last ldc, 2 ldc in last ldc. Ch 3, turn. 60 (64, 67, 72, 78, 83) ldc.

Row 5 Rep Row 3.

Rows 6–11 Rep Rows 2–3 3 times. 66 (70, 73, 78, 84, 89) ldc after Row 10.

Work even if needed until Sleeve measures 7 (7, 7, 8, 8, 8) in. from beg.

SHAPE SLEEVE CAP

Row 1 Sl st in each of 1st 7 (8, 9, 10, 10, 10) ldc, ch 3 (counts as 1 ldc), ldc in each ldc across until 6 (7, 8, 9, 9, 9) ldc remain. Ch 3, turn. 54 (56, 57, 60, 66, 73) ldc.

Row 2 Ldc2tog, ldc in each ldc across to last 2 sts, ldc2tog. Ch 3, turn. 52 (54, 55, 58, 64, 71) ldc.

Rows 3–5 Rep Row 2. 46 (48, 49, 52, 58, 65) ldc after Row 5.

Row 6 Ldc in each ldc across. Ch 3, turn.

Row 7 Rep Row 2. 44 (46, 47, 50, 56, 63) ldc. Sizes L and XL only, go to Row 10.

Rows 8-9 (9, 11, 13) Rep Rows 6–7 1 (1, 2, 3) time(s). 45 (48, 52, 57) ldc.

Rows 10-11 Rep Row 6.

Row 12 Rep Row 2. 42 (44, 43, 46, 50, 55) ldc.

Row 13 Sl st in each of 1st 3 ldc, sc, hdc, ldc across until 5 ldc remain, hdc, sc, sl st. Ch 1, turn. 36 (38, 37, 40, 48, 49) sts, not counting sl sts.

Row 14 Sl st in each of 1st 5 sts, sc, hdc, ldc across until 7 sts remain, hdc, sc, sl st. Ch 1, turn. 26 (28, 27, 30, 38, 39) sts, not counting sl sts.

Row 15 Rep Row 14. 16 (18, 17, 20, 28, 29) sts, not counting sl sts. Sizes L (XL, 2X, 3X) only, end off.

Sizes 4X (5X) only:

Row 16 Rep Row 14. End off. 18 (19) sts, not counting sl sts.

Assembly

Block pieces if desired.

Sew Fronts to Back at shoulders. Sew underarm seam of Sleeves. Insert Sleeves into openings and sew in place.

Button Band

Row 1 With RS of assembled garment facing, sctbl across 1st ribbing section, sc evenly up 1st front, around neckline, and down 2nd front, sctbl across final ribbing section. Ch 1, turn.

Row 2 Sctbl across 1st 15 sc, sc in each sc across until 15 sts remain, sctbl in each sc to end. Ch 1, turn. Count scs along the section of Right Front below the start of the neck edge decreases. Plan the buttonholes using the formula from the Essential Cardigan on p. 68.

Row 3 Stitch buttonholes as planned, sc in each sc around to end of row. Ch 1, turn.

Row 4 Sc in each sc, 2 sc in each ch-2 sp across. Ch 1, turn.

Row 5 Sc in each sc across. End off.

Weave in all ends. Sew buttons to button band, opposite buttonholes.

continued on page 80

Comely Cardigan Schematics

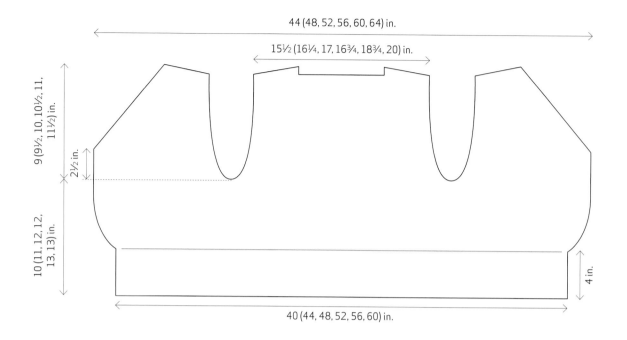

44 (48, 52, 56, 60, 64) in.

15½ (16¼, 17, 16¾, 18¾, 20) in.

9 (9½, 10, 10½, 11, 11½) in.

2½ in.

10 (11, 12, 12, 13, 13) in.

4 in.

40 (44, 48, 52, 56, 60) in.

SLEEVE

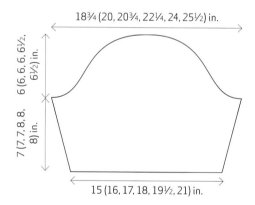

18¾ (20, 20¾, 22¼, 24, 25½) in.

6 (6, 6, 6, 6½, 6½) in.

7 (7, 7, 8, 8, 8) in.

15 (16, 17, 18, 19½, 21) in.

Simply Stripes Jacket

Comfortable does not have to mean bulky. This soft wool jacket, made in a DK weight yarn, has a relaxed fit but still looks put together. Some garments with an open front are unflattering on the plus-size figure because the sides form an A or a V shape, pointing to your widest feature. To avoid that look, arrange the wide lacy collar as you need to in order to keep the front edges hanging straight.

Tip: This sweater is stitched from side to side, so if you want to change the length of the garment, you need to make changes in the number of stitches, not the number of rows. You can increase or decrease the width by adding or subtracting "stripes."

SKILL LEVEL
Easy

FINISHED BUST
L (XL, 2X, 3X, 4X, 5X); 45 (50, 55, 60, 65, 70) in. *Garment is not meant to close in front.*

YARN
Valley Yarns Northfield; 5 (6, 6, 7, 7, 8) skeins Black (Color A); 3 (3, 4, 4, 5, 5) skeins each Red (Color B), Charcoal (Color C), and Haze (Color D); and 2 (2, 3, 3, 4, 4) skeins Natural (Color E) (50 g/124 yds); 1,984 (2,108, 2,604, 2,728, 3,224, 3,348) yds DK weight yarn (CYCA 3, Light, see p. 146)

NOTIONS
Hook size H/8 U.S. (5 mm) *or size needed to obtain gauge* 2 hooks sizes I/9 U.S. (5.5 mm) and J/10 U.S. (6 mm) for collar only, or the next two hook sizes larger than the gauge hook
Stitch marker
Tapestry needle

GAUGE
12 sts and 12 rows (4 stripes) = 4 in. in patt st

NOTES
Ch-3 counts as 1 dc throughout.
Ch-4 counts as 1 dc plus ch-1 sp throughout.
Color sequence for stripes is: *B, C, D, A, E, A, D, C, B, A. Rep from * throughout piece. Always change color before the t-ch for the new color row.

Sleeve (Make 2)

With Color A, ch 52 (52, 58, 58, 66, 66).
Row 1 Sc in 2nd ch from hook and in each ch across. Ch 1, turn. 51 (51, 57, 57, 65, 65) sts.
Row 2 Sc in each sc across. Ch 3, turn.
Row 3 Dc in each sc across. Ch 1, turn.
Row 4 Sc in each dc across. Change to Color B, ch 1, turn.
Rep Rows 2–4 twice, changing colors after every repeat following the color sequence in the Notes.

INCREASE FOR SLEEVE

Row 1 2 sc in 1st sc, sc in each dc across to last dc, 2 sc in last dc. Ch 3, turn. 53 (53, 59, 59, 67, 67) sts.
Row 2 Dc in each sc across. Ch 1, turn.
Row 3 2 sc in 1st dc, sc in each dc across to last dc, 2 sc in last dc. Ch 3, turn. 55 (55, 61, 61, 69, 69) sts.
Rows 4–30 Rep Rows 1–3, maintaining color sequence as established. 91 (91, 97, 97, 105, 105) sts.

continued on page 83

SLEEVE CAP SHAPING

Row 1 Sl st in each of 1st 3 sts, sc across until 3 sts remain. Ch 3, turn. 85 (85, 91, 91, 99, 99) sts.

Row 2 Dc2tog, dc across until 2 sts remain, dc2tog. Ch 1, turn. 83 (83, 89, 89, 97, 97) sts.

Row 3 Sc2tog, dc across until 2 sts remain, sc2tog. Ch 3, turn. 81 (81, 87, 87, 95, 95) sts (change to next color in the sequence).

Row 4 Rep Row 3. 79 (79, 85, 85, 93, 93) sts.

Rows 5–6 Rep Rows 2–3. 75 (75, 81, 81, 89, 89) sts.

Sizes L (XL, 2X, 3X) only:
End off.

Sizes 4X (5X) only:

Row 7 Rep Row 3. 87 (87) sts.

Rows 8–9 Rep Rows 2–3. End off. 83 (83) sts.

Front and Back Set-Ups (Make 4)

With Color A, ch 43 (43, 52, 52, 55, 55).

Row 1 Sc in 2nd ch from hook and in each ch across. Ch 3, turn. 42 (42, 51, 51, 55, 55) sts.

Row 2 Dc in each sc across. Ch 1, turn.

Row 3 Sc in each dc across. Ch 1, turn.

Continuing in Color A, rep Rows 1–3 for pattern 1 (1, 1, 1, 2, 2) time(s). End off.

Jacket Right Half

Line up 2 Set-Ups so that there is one on either side of a Sleeve, with the same sides of the work facing you. Attach the next color in the stripe sequence for the Sleeve in the 1st st of the 1st Set-Up. Ch 1, do not turn.

Row 1 Sc in each sc across the 1st Set-Up, Sleeve, and the 2nd Set-up. Ch 3, turn. 159 (159, 183, 183, 193, 193) sts.

Row 2 Dc in each sc across, ch 1, turn.

Row 3 Sc in each dc across, change to next color in sequence, ch 1, turn.

Rep Rows 1–3 for pattern until work measures 4 (5, 6, 7, 8, 9) in. from Row 1, ending with a Row 3.

Divide for Front and Back

BACK

Row 1 77 (77, 89, 89, 94, 94) sc across, leaving rem sts unworked, ch 3, turn.

Row 2 Dc in each sc across. Ch 1, turn.

Row 3 Sc in each dc across to neck opening, change color. Ch 1, turn.

Row 4 Sc in each sc across, ch 3, turn.

Rows 5–6 Rep Rows 2–3.

Rep Rows 4–6 following the stripe sequence for pattern, until work measures 7 (8, 9, 10, 11, 12) in. from Divide, ending with a Row 6. End off.

FRONT

Row 1 Continuing in the same direction and with the same color as the 1st row of the Back, from last Back st, sk 9 sc, join with sc in next st, and sc in each of next 4 sts, place marker in st just worked, sc in each sc across. Ch 3, turn. 73 (73, 85, 85, 90, 90).

Row 2 Dc in each dc across to marked st, remove marker, hdc in each of next 2 sc, sc in each of last 3 sc, ch 1, turn.

Row 3 Sl st in each of 1st 5 sts, ch 1, sc2tog, place marker in st just worked, sc in each sc to end. Change to next color in the stripe sequence, ch 1, turn. 67 (67, 79, 79, 84, 84) sc.

Row 4 Sc in each sc across to st before marked st, sc2tog, ch 1, turn. 66 (66, 78, 78, 83, 83) sc.

Row 5 Sl st in 1st sc, sc in each of next 2 sc, hdc in each of next 2 sc, dc in each sc to end, placing marker in 1st dc worked. Ch 1, turn. 61 (61, 73, 73, 78, 78) dc.

Row 6 Sc in each sc across to st before marked st, sc2tog. Change to next color in the stripe sequence, ch 1, turn. 60 (60, 72, 72, 77, 77) sc.

Row 7 Sc2tog, sc in each of next 4 sts, place marker, sc in each sc across. Ch 3, turn. 59 (59, 71, 71, 76, 76) sc.

Rows 8–12 Rep Rows 2–6. End off. 46 (46, 58, 55, 63, 63) sc.

Jacket Left Half

Rep instructions for the Right Half of the jacket.

At end of Back instructions, add 1 more stripe (3 more rows) in the next color in the sequence.

Assembly

Block all pieces.

Using whip st, seam the shaped part of sleeve cap to corresponding sts on Front and Back.

Using whip st, stitch the front pieces to the back and sleeve edges, together with one seam from the hem of the jacket to the hem of each sleeve.

Using whip st, stitch the two halves of the jacket together at the Back seam.

Collar

With RS facing, and beginning at the bottom of the opening, work 1 row sc using hook size H/8 U.S.

continued on page 84

(5 mm) and Color A, evenly spacing the sts along the front opening, the neck edge of the back, and the next front opening to the opposite hem, making sure to make an odd number of sts. Ch 1, turn.

Row 1 Change to hook size I/9 U.S. (5.5 mm) and sc in each sc across. Ch 4, turn.

Row 2 Sk 1st dc, dc in next dc, *ch 1, sk 1 dc, dc in next dc. Rep from * to end. Ch 1, turn.

Row 3 Sc in each dc and ch-1 sp across. Ch 4, turn.

Rep Rows 2–3 one more time using the size I/9 U.S. (5.5 mm) hook, then rep Rows 2–3 using the size J/10 U.S. (6 mm) hook until the collar measures 6 in. or the desired length, ending with a Row 3. End off.

Bottom Edge Detail

Row 1 With Color A and RS facing, and using the size H/8 U.S. (5 mm) hook, work one row of sc evenly spaced across the bottom edge of the assembled jacket. Ch 3, turn.

Row 2 Dc in each sc across. Ch 1, turn.

Row 3 Sc in each dc across. End off if desired, or work as many 3-row groups (sc, dc, sc) as you wish to adjust the total garment length.

Weave in all ends.

Simply Stripes Jacket Schematics

RIGHT HALF AND LEFT HALF

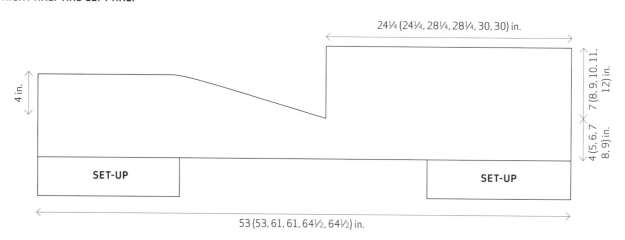

SLEEVE

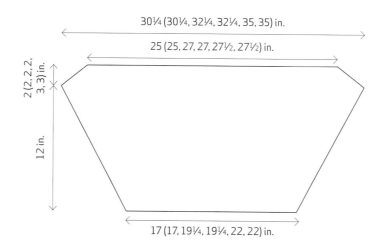

While the model shown used high-contrast colors for a lot of punch, you could easily substitute more subtle color combinations. If the shape of the garment appeals to you but you are not big on stripes, just make it all in one color!

Intertwined Poncho

Fads in fashion may come and go, but simple ponchos with clean lines never go out of style. Ponchos are excellent pieces to put in your outerwear collection, as they add a moderate amount of warmth, perfect for many seasons.

Tip: This piece is easily customizable. To make it longer or shorter in length, add or subtract stitches to the width of the panel between the cables; to change the circumference, add or subtract rows to the length of the panel by continuing the pattern repeat as needed.

SKILL LEVEL

Intermediate. *Cabling makes this an intermediate-level pattern, but if you can handle back and front post stitching, you can definitely complete this project!*

FINISHED SIZE

One size: 20 x 33 in. per panel

YARN

Lion Brand® Yarn Wool-Ease®; 5 skeins Seaspray, #620-123 (3 oz/197 yds); 985 yds worsted weight yarn (CYCA 4, Medium, see p. 146)

NOTIONS

Hook size I/9 U.S. (5.5 mm) *or size needed to obtain gauge*
Tapestry needle

GAUGE

11 sts and 10 rows = 4 in. in hdc

NOTES

Ch-2 counts as 1 hdc throughout.
Back post double crochet (bpdc) and front post double crochet (fpdc) stitches are abbreviated throughout. For a list of all abbreviations used in this book, see Hook Sizing and Abbreviations, p. 144.

Panel (Make 2)

Ch 61.

Row 1 Hdc in 3rd ch from hook and in each ch across. Ch 2, turn. 60 hdc (ch-2 counts as 1 hdc here and throughout).

Row 2 (WS) Hdc in next hdc, bpdc in each of next 6 hdc, hdc in each hdc across until 8 hdc remain, bpdc in each of next 6 hdc, hdc in each of last 2 hdc. Ch 2, turn.

Row 3 (RS) Hdc in next hdc, {sk 2 bpdc, fpdc in each of next 2 bpdc, fpdc in each of 2 skipped bpdc, fpdc in each of last 2 bpdc in this group}, hdc in each hdc across, rep instructions in { }, hdc in each of last 2 hdc. Ch 2, turn.

Row 4 and all even rows Hdc in next hdc, bpdc in each of next 6 fpdc, hdc in each hdc across, bpdc in each of next 6 fpdc, hdc in each of last 2 hdc. Ch 2, turn.

Row 5 Hdc in next hdc, {fpdc in each of next 2 bpdc, sk 2 bpdc, fpdc in each of next 2 bpdc, fpdc in each of 2 skipped bpdc}, hdc in each hdc across, rep instructions in { }, hdc in each of last 2 hdc.

Rep Rows 3–6 for pattern until work measures 33 in., ending with a Row 6. End off.

Cable Trim Piece (Make 2)

Ch 10.

Row 1 Hdc in 3rd ch from hook and in each ch across. Ch 2, turn. 9 hdc.

Row 2 (WS) Hdc in next hdc, bpdc in each of next 6 hdc, hdc in last hdc. Ch 2, turn.

Row 3 Hdc in next hdc, sk 2 bpdc, fpdc in each of next 2 bpdc, fpdc in each of 2 skipped bpdc, fpdc in each of last 2 bpdc in this group, hdc in last hdc. Ch 2, turn.

continued on page 89

Cables in crochet are a
lot easier to make than
they look, being a simple
repeat of front and back
post stitches. They add
a neat, tailored style to
any project.

Row 4 and all remaining even rows Hdc in next hdc, bpdc in each of next 6 fpdc, hdc in last hdc. Ch 2, turn.

Row 5 Hdc in next hdc, fpdc in each of next 2 bpdc, sk 2 bpdc, fpdc in each of next 2 bpdc, fpdc in each of 2 skipped bpdc, hdc in last hdc. Ch 2, turn.

Rep Rows 3–6 until work measures 20 in. or width of Panel, ending with a Row 6. End off.

Assembly

Lay both panels next to each other, short sides toward you with right sides facing up.

Stitch one Cable Trim Piece to the bottom of the Panel on your right, placing the side with 1 hdc closest to the panel. The side with 2 hdc is now the bottom edge.

Stitch the remaining Cable Trim Piece to the top of the Panel on your left, placing the side with 1 hdc closest to the panel. The side with 2 hdc in now the top edge.

Rotate the left Panel 90 degrees to the left. Line up the pieces so that the new bottom edge of the left Panel is even with the bottom edge of the right Panel. Stitch the pieces together where they meet.

Fold the right Panel so that the top right edge meets the top left edge of the left Panel. Stitch the pieces together where they meet.

Weave in all ends.

Intertwined Poncho Schematic

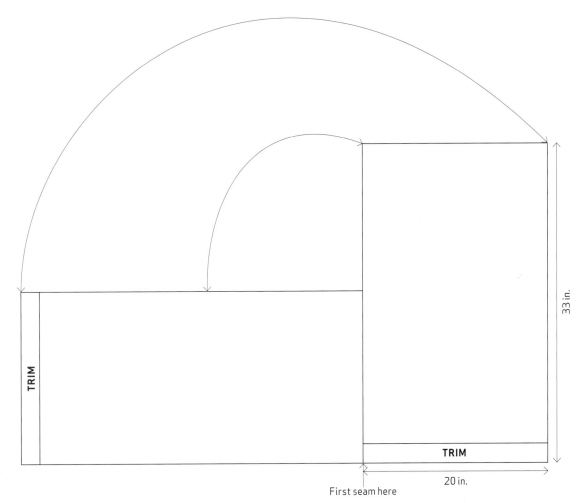

TRIM

TRIM

33 in.

20 in.

First seam here

Peacoat for Rule Breakers

This comfy coat is one of those exceptions that proves the rules! While I normally don't advocate bulky-weight yarns for plus-size projects, sometimes we all need a quick-to-stitch project for that instant gratification fix. Don't be afraid of using thicker yarns for outerwear. If you can't find a bulky yarn that you love, experiment with holding together multiple strands of your favorite worsted or even DK weight yarn and stitching them as one.

Tip: Wait until you try the coat on to finalize the pocket placement to put them in the most flattering place. This is one of those small details that will make your garment look its very best on you.

SKILL LEVEL
Beginner

FINISHED BUST
L (XL, 2X, 3X, 4X, 5X); 50 (54, 58, 62, 66, 70) in., *buttoned for an oversized fit*

YARN
Premier Yarns Serenity Chunky Tweeds; 12 (13, 13, 14, 15, 16) skeins Cypress, #DN900-04 (3.5 oz/109 yds); 1,308 (1,417, 1,417, 1,526, 1,635, 1,744) yds chunky weight yarn (CYCA 5, Bulky, see p. 146)

NOTIONS
Hook sizes M/N-13 U.S. (9 mm) and N/P-15 U.S. (10 mm) *or size needed to obtain gauge*
2 stitch markers
11 (11, 11, 12, 12, 12) buttons, 1½ in. in diameter

GAUGE
6 sts and 5 rows = 4 in. in hdc with larger hook

NOTES
The sleeve length in the schematic may seem long, but that's not a typo: The sleeves are stitched at a longer-than-necessary length so you can fold back a generous cuff.
Ch-2 counts as 1 hdc.
For crab stitch instructions, see Techniques and Stitches, p. 141.

Back

With larger hook, ch 39 (42, 45, 48, 51, 54).
Row 1 Hdc in 3rd ch from hook and in each ch across. Ch 2, turn. 38 (41, 44, 47, 50, 53) hdc.
Row 2 (RS) Hdc in each hdc across (ch-2 counts as 1 hdc here and throughout). Ch 2, turn.
Work even, repeating Row 2 for pattern until 30 rows have been completed. Ch 1, turn.

ARMHOLE SHAPING

Row 1 Sl st in each of 3 (3, 4, 4, 5, 5) hdc, ch 2, hdc in each hdc across until 2 (2, 3, 3, 4, 4) sts remain. Ch 1, turn. 34 (37, 38, 41, 42, 45) hdc.
Row 2 Hdc2tog, hdc in each hdc across until 2 sts remain, hdc2tog. Ch 2, turn. 32 (35, 36, 39, 40, 43) hdc.
Rep Row 2 2 (3, 3, 4, 4, 5) more times. 28 (29, 30, 31, 32, 33) hdc after the final repeat.
Work even on these sts (hdc in each hdc across) if necessary, until work measures 10 (10, 10, 12, 12, 12) in. from start of Armhole Shaping, ch 1, turn after last row.

continued on page 92

FIRST SHOULDER

Row 1 Sl st in each of 1st 2 (2, 2, 3, 3, 3) hdc, sc in each of next 2 hdc, hdc in each of next 2 hdc, dc in each of next 2 hdc. End off yarn.

SECOND SHOULDER

Row 1 Working in the same direction as Row 1 of First Shoulder, sk 12 (13, 14, 13, 14, 15) hdc, attach yarn in next hdc, ch 3 (counts as 1 dc), dc in next hdc, hdc in each of next 2 hdc, sc in each of next 2 hdc. End off.

Right Front with Buttonholes

With larger hook ch 23 (25, 26, 28, 29, 31).
Row 1 (RS) Hdc in 3rd ch from hook and in each ch across. Ch 2, turn. 22 (24, 25, 27, 28, 30).
Rows 2–4 Hdc in each hdc across. Ch 2, turn.
Row 5 2 hdc, ch 1, sk 1 hdc, hdc in next hdc and in each hdc across. Ch 2, turn.
Row 6 Hdc in each hdc and ch-1 sp across. Ch 2, turn.
Rows 7–10 Rep Row 2.
Rep Rows 5–10 3 times, then Rows 5–6 once more.

ARMHOLE SHAPING

Row 1 Hdc in each hdc across until 2 (2, 3, 3, 4, 4) sts remain. Ch 2, turn. 20 (22, 22, 24, 24, 26) hdc.
Row 2 Hdc2tog, hdc in each hdc to end. Ch 2, turn. 19 (21, 21, 23, 23, 25) hdc.
Row 3 Hdc in each hdc across until 2 sts remain, hdc2tog. Ch 2, turn. 18 (20, 20, 22, 22, 24) hdc.
Row 4 Rep Row 2. 17 (19, 19, 21, 21, 23) hdc.
Row 5 2 hdc, ch 1, sk 1 hdc, hdc in next hdc and in each hdc across. Ch 2, turn.
Row 6 Hdc in each hdc and ch-1 sp across. Ch 2, turn.

NECKLINE SHAPING

Row 1 Sl st in each of 4 (6, 6, 5, 5, 7) hdc, ch 2, hdc2tog, hdc in each hdc to end. Ch 2, turn. 13 (13, 13, 16, 16, 16) hdc.
Row 2 Hdc in each hdc across until 2 sts remain, hdc2tog. Ch 2, turn. 12 (12, 12, 15, 15, 15) hdc.
Row 3 Hdc2tog, hdc in each hdc to end. Ch 2, turn. 11 (11, 11, 14, 14, 14) hdc.
Rows 4–6 (6, 6, 8, 8, 8) Rep Rows 2–3 1 (1, 1, 2, 2, 2) time(s), then Row 2 once more. Ch 3, turn after Row 6 (6, 6, 8, 8, 8). 8 (8, 8, 9, 9, 9) hdc.

SHOULDER SHAPING

Row 1 Dc in next hdc, hdc in each of next 2 hdc, sc in each of next 2 hdc. End off.

Left Front

Rep instructions for Right Front up to Armhole Shaping, ch 1, turn at end of last row.

ARMHOLE SHAPING

Row 1 Sl st in each of 3 (3, 4, 4, 5, 5) hdc, ch 2, hdc in each hdc across. Ch 2, turn. 20 (22, 22, 24, 24, 26) hdc.
Row 2 Hdc in each hdc across until 2 sts remain, hdc2tog. Ch 2, turn. 19 (21, 21, 23, 23, 25) hdc.
Row 3 Hdc2tog, hdc in each hdc to end. Ch 2, turn. 18 (20, 20, 22, 22, 24) hdc.
Rows 4–6 Hdc in each hdc across. Ch 2, turn.

NECKLINE SHAPING

Row 1 Hdc in each hdc across until 6 (8, 8, 7, 7, 9) sts remain, hdc2tog, hdc. Ch 2, turn. 13 (13, 13, 16, 16, 16) hdc.
Row 2 Hdc2tog, hdc in each hdc across. Ch 2, turn. 12 (12, 12, 15, 15, 15) hdc.
Row 3 Hdc in each hdc across until 2 sts remain, hdc2tog. Ch 2, turn. 11 (11, 11, 14, 14, 14) hdc.
Rows 4–6 (6, 6, 8, 8, 8) Rep Rows 2–3 1 (1, 1, 2, 2, 2) times, then Row 2 once more. Ch 3, turn after Row 6 (6, 6, 8, 8, 8). 8 (8, 8, 9, 9, 9) hdc.

SHOULDER SHAPING

Row 1 Sl st in each of 1st 2 (2, 2, 3, 3, 3) hdc, sc in each of next 2 hdc, hdc in each of next 2 hdc, dc in each of next 2 hdc. End off.

Sleeve (Make 2)

With smaller hook, ch 21 (21, 24, 24, 27, 27).
Row 1 Hdc in 3rd ch from hook and in each ch across. 20 (20, 23, 23, 26, 26) hdc. Ch 2, turn.
Row 2 Hdc in each hdc across, ch 2, turn.
Rows 3–5 Work even by repeating Row 2.
Rows 6–11 Change to larger hook, work even by repeating Row 2.
Row 12 Hdc in 1st hdc (inc when paired with ch-2) and in each hdc across to last hdc, 2 hdc in last hdc. Ch 2, turn. 22 (22, 25, 25, 28, 28) hdc.
Rows 13–16 Work even.
Rep Rows 13–16 2 more times, then Row 12 once more. 28 (28, 31, 31, 34, 34) hdc.
Work even if needed until work measures 21 (21, 23, 23, 25, 25) in. from beg, ch 1, turn after final row.

Row 1 Sl st in each of 3 (3, 4, 4, 5, 5) hdc, ch 2, hdc in each hdc across until 2 (2, 3, 3, 4, 4) sts remain. Ch 1, turn. 24 (24, 25, 25, 26, 26) hdc.

Row 2 Hdc2tog, hdc in each hdc across until 2 sts remain, hdc2tog. Ch 2, turn. 22 (22, 23, 23, 24, 24) hdc.

Rows 3–4 Rep Row 2. 18 (18, 19, 19, 20, 20) hdc.

Row(s) 5 (5, 5, 5–7, 5–7, 5–7) Work even.

Rows 6 (6, 6, 8, 8, 8)–7 (7, 7, 9, 9, 9) Rep Row 2, ch 1, after last row. 14 (14, 15, 15, 16, 16) hdc.

Last Row Sl st in each of 1st 2 (2, 2, 2, 3, 3) hdc, sc in each of next 2 hdc, hdc in each of next 6 (6, 6, 6, 7, 7) hdc, sc in each of next 2 hdc, sl st in each of last 2 (2, 2, 2, 3, 3) hdc. End off.

Patch Pocket (Make 2)

With larger hook, ch 11.

Row 1 Sc in 2nd ch from hook and in each ch across. Ch 1, turn. 10 sc.

Row 2 Sc in each sc across. Ch 1, turn.

Rows 3–12 Rep Row 2, do not turn, do not end off after Row 12.

Edging

With larger hook, work crab st around the pocket, placing 10 sts on each side. End off.

Hood

With larger hook, ch 28 (28, 28, 33, 33, 33).

Row 1 Hdc in 3rd ch from hook and in each ch across. Ch 2, turn. 27 (27, 27, 32, 32, 32) hdc.

Row 2 3 hdc, (ch 1, sk 1 hdc, 4 hdc) 4 (4, 4, 5, 5, 5) times, ch 1, sk 1 hdc, 3 hdc. Ch 2, turn.

Row 3 Hdc in each hdc and ch-1 sp across. Ch 2, turn.

Row 4 Hdc in each of 8 (8, 8, 9, 9, 9) hdc, 3 hdc in next hdc, place marker in center st of those 3, hdc in each of next 9 (9, 9, 12, 12, 12) hdc, 3 hdc in next hdc, place marker at center st of those 3, hdc in each hdc to end. Ch 2, turn. 31 (31, 31, 36, 36, 36) hdc.

Row 5 Work even.

Row 6 (Hdc in each hdc to marked st, 3 hdc in marked st, mark center st of those 3) twice, hdc in each hdc to end. Ch 2, turn. 35 (35, 35, 40, 40, 40) hdc.

Row 7 Work even.

Rows 8–13 Rep Row 6–7 3 times. 47 (47, 47, 52, 52, 52) hdc.

Rows 14–15 (15, 15, 18, 18, 18) Work even.

Row 1 (Hdc to st before marked st, hdc3tog) twice, hdc to end. Ch 2, turn. 43 (43, 43, 48, 48, 48).

Row 2 Work even.

Rep Rows 1–2 until 7 (7, 7, 8, 8, 8) hdc remain. End off, leaving a long tail for sewing.

Fold top of hood in half, whip st 1st 3 (3, 3, 4, 4, 4) sts to last 4 sts.

Assembly

With larger hook, work 1 rnd crab st all the way around completed hood.

Sew Fronts to Back at shoulders and side seams.

Sew Sleeve underarm seams, and stitch each Sleeve into place.

Row 1 With RS facing and starting at 1st st of 1st dec row of Right Front, work 34 (39, 40, 41, 42, 47) hdc evenly spaced around entire neckline, finishing at the last st opposite. Ch 2, turn.

Rows 2–4 Hdc in each hdc across. End off after Row 4. Work 1 rnd crab st around each Sleeve hem and fold them back to desired length.

Finish

Work 1 rnd crab st around entire coat body, including bottom hem, front openings, and neckline.

Sew buttons opposite buttonholes on the coat and around the collar opposite the buttonholes on the hood.

Stitch patch pockets into place.

Weave in all ends.

continued on page 94

Peacoat for Rule Breakers Schematics

BACK

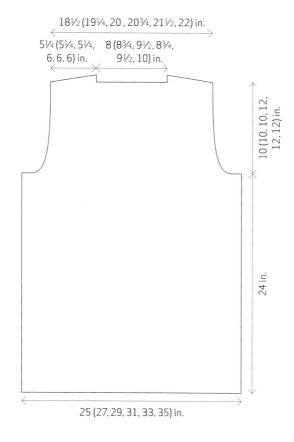

18½ (19¼, 20 , 20¾, 21½, 22) in.

5¼ (5¼, 5¼, 6, 6, 6) in.

8 (8¾, 9½, 8¾, 9½, 10) in.

10 (10, 10, 12, 12, 12) in.

24 in.

25 (27, 29, 31, 33, 35) in.

FRONTS

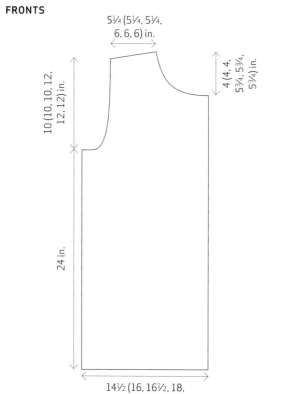

5¼ (5¼, 5¼, 6, 6, 6) in.

4 (4, 4, 5¾, 5¾, 5¾) in.

10 (10, 10, 12, 12) in.

24 in.

14½ (16, 16½, 18, 18¾, 20) in.

SLEEVE

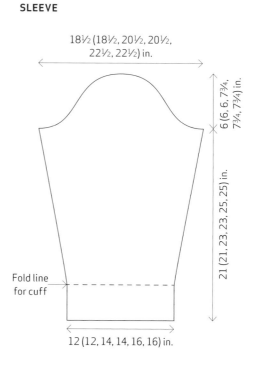

18½ (18½, 20½, 20½, 22½, 22½) in.

6 (6, 6, 7¾, 7¾, 7¾) in.

21 (21, 23, 23, 25, 25) in.

Fold line for cuff

12 (12, 14, 14, 16, 16) in.

By placing gorgeous buttons on the outside of the stand-up collar, you can take advantage of them as decoration whether the detachable hood is attached or not.

Traditional Cloak

This pattern is written a little differently than others in the book—it's more like a recipe that allows you to customize your fit as you go. The cloak is crocheted from the neck down, so you will try on the garment as you work and make adjustments to find just the right drape and length for your body. Add or subtract increase rows to adjust the amount of fullness, and check the length as you stitch to create anything from a capelet to a floor-length, swirling masterpiece!

Tip: Plain double crochet not for you? Try the linked double crochet stitch pattern (p. 140) or grab a double crochet–based diagram from your favorite stitch dictionary and experiment.

SKILL LEVEL
Easy

FINISHED LENGTH
Sample size: 40 in. from neck to bottom edge. *Try on the cloak as you go and stop when you are happy with the fit.*

YARN
Red Heart Super Saver®; for sample shown, 7 skeins soft Navy, #0387 (7 oz/364 yds); yardage will vary depending on finished size and gauge (CYCA 4, Medium, see p. 146)

NOTIONS
Hook size I/9 U.S. (5.5 mm) *or size needed to obtain gauge*
5 stitch markers
2 leather S-style closures, or decorative frog closures of your choice
Sewing needle and thread
Tapestry needle

GAUGE
Sample gauge: 10 sts and 6 rows = 4 in. in dc. *Gauge not critical for pattern.*

NOTE
For crab stitch instructions, see Techniques and Stitches, p. 141.

Cloak

Ch any multiple of 6 plus 1. The ch should fit comfortably around your neck. For the sample, ch 61.
Row 1 Take the number of multiples of 6 you chained, minus 1. That number is X: Dc in 4th ch from hook and in each of next (X − 2) ch, *(dc, ch 1, dc) in next ch, dc in each of next X ch. Rep from * to end. Ch 3, turn. For the sample, dc in 4th ch from hook and in each of next 7 ch, *(dc, ch 1, dc) in next ch, dc in each of next 9 ch. Rep from * to end.
Row 2 Dc in each dc to ch-1 sp, *3 dc in ch-1 sp, dc in each dc to ch-1 sp. Place marker in the center dc of 3-dc increase. Rep from * to end. Ch 3, turn.
Row 3 Dc in each dc to marked st, *3 dc in marked st, place marker in the center dc of 3-dc increase, dc in each dc to marked st. Rep from * to end. Ch 3, turn.
Rep Row 3 until work measures 5 in. more than your shoulder-to-shoulder width measurement, taken from the outside of your arm to the outside of the opposite arm. Measure the work across the whole top of the cloak, laid flat. For the sample, Rep Row 3 until work measures 30 in.

continued on page 98

Alternate working Row 3 (increase row) and a work even row until work measures the desired length along the straight edge, from collar to top of arm slit, ending with an even row. For the sample, work until work measures 17 in.

DIVIDE FOR ARM SLITS

Dc in each dc to st before marked st, 2 dc in st before marked st, sk marked st, with new ball of yarn 2 dc in next dc, *dc in each dc to marked st, 3 dc in marked st. Rep from * 2 more times, dc in each dc to st before marked st, 2 dc in st before marked st, sk marked st, with new ball of yarn 2 dc in next dc, dc in each dc to end. Ch 3, turn.

Work Fronts and Back separately as follows.

FIRST FRONT

Dc in each dc to end of section, 2 dc in last sc. Ch 3, turn.

Alternate this increase row with a work even row until slit measures desired height, ending with a work even row. For the sample, work until slit measures 10 in.

BACK

2 dc in first dc, *dc in each dc to marked dc, 3 dc in marked dc, place marker in center dc of 3-dc increase. Rep from * to end of section, dc in each dc to last dc, 2 dc in last dc. Ch 3, turn.

Alternate this increase row with a work even row until slit measures same height as First Front, ending with a work even row. For the sample, work until slit measures 10 in.

SECOND FRONT

2 dc in 1st dc of section, dc in each dc to end. Ch 3, turn. Alternate this increase row with a work even row until slit measures same height as First Front, ending with a work even row. For the sample, work until slit measures 10 in.

JOIN FRONTS AND BACK

Dc in each dc to end of First Front, 3 dc in last dc, place marker in the center dc of 3-dc increase, working across Back, *dc in each dc to marked dc, 3 dc in marked dc, place marker in center dc of 3-dc increase. Rep from * to end, dc in each dc to end of Back, 3 dc in last dc, mark center dc of 3-dc increase, dc in each dc of Second Front to end, ch 3, turn.

Alternate work even rows and original increase rows (Row 3) until Cloak measures desired length. For less fullness at the hem, simply work even to desired length. End off. For the sample, work until Cloak measures 40 in.

Finish

If desired, add a collar, an edging up the fronts and on the hem, closures, and/or decorative accents on the arm slits. Sample has a stand-up collar made by working 3 rows of dc on the opposite side of the foundation ch, a crab st edging around the entire garment, and a contrast faux-welt on the arm slits made by working 3 rnds of dc around the rectangular arm slit and placing a (dc, ch 1, dc) increase in each corner.

Weave in ends. Add your desired closure. Tack down the outer edges of the arm slit welt if you made them.

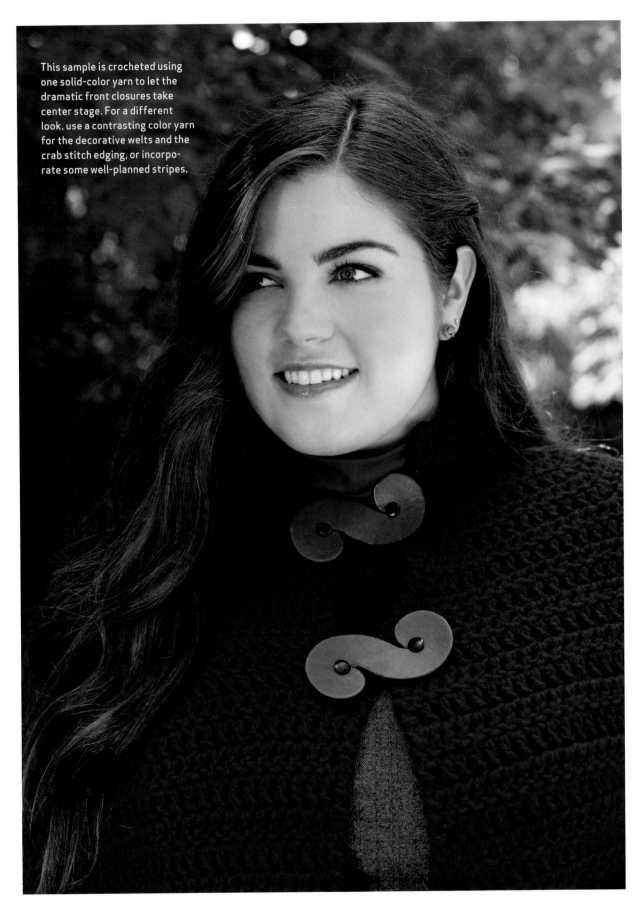

This sample is crocheted using one solid-color yarn to let the dramatic front closures take center stage. For a different look, use a contrasting color yarn for the decorative welts and the crab stitch edging, or incorporate some well-planned stripes.

CHAPTER
5

Wraps, Bags, and Accessories

WHILE WRAPS AND ACCESSORIES DON'T NEED TO FIT OUR BODIES in the same way that fitted garments do, they do need to fit in with our overall look—a bag such as the Carryall (p. 127) carried by a size 22 and a size 2 will not have the same visual effect on both women: One has a colorful, fun accessory; the other is overwhelmed by a too-big bag!

Accessories for the plus-size woman are about being comfortable, being stylish, and using their textures, shapes, and colors to add to our overall look, rather than being an afterthought.

Pieces such as the Sensible Shawl (p. 114) and the Stratum Wrap (p. 102) work because although they are large pieces of fabric, they are crocheted in lightweight yarns that add color without bulk. But you don't need an accessory to be large to work for your body. The smallest scarf, Shimmer Scarf (p. 124), is a dressy confection of silk and sequins that offers an impact far larger than its actual size.

Accessories also have the advantage of being quick to make, and they do not require a ton of modifications in the stitching. Make several to keep in your closet to dress up any outfit.

Stratum Wrap

The many layers of color in this wrap really stack up. Stratum is an exercise in geometry! The fronts are rectangles, the center back and embellishments are wedges, and the long color repeat of the yarn adds softly shifting stripes. Fold the fabric like a scarf and slip it over or under your coat collar, or wear it as a wrap to jazz up a plain outfit with the addition of a shawl pin.

Tip: Dense stitch patterns allow a lightweight yarn to give you lots of warmth without adding too much bulk to a garment.

SKILL LEVEL
Easy

FINISHED SIZE
Fronts: 24 x 14 in. *without wedge trim*

YARN
Crystal Palace Mini Mochi; 6 skeins Jungle, #110 (50 g/195 yds); 1,170 yds fingering weight yarn (CYCA 1, Super Fine, see p. 146)

NOTIONS
Hook size F/5 U.S. (3.75 mm) *or size needed to obtain gauge*
Tapestry needle

GAUGE
18 sts and 10 rows = 4 in. in patt st

NOTE
Ch-3 counts as 1 dc throughout.

Front (Make 2)
Loosely ch 110.
Row 1 Sc in 2nd ch from hook, *sk 2 ch, 5 dc in next ch, sk 2 ch, sc in next ch. Rep from * to end, placing last sc in last ch. Ch 3, turn. 18 5-dc shells.
Row 2 2 dc in 1st sc, sk 2 dc, sc in next dc, *5 dc in next sc, sk 2 dc, sc in next dc. Rep from * to end, 3 dc in last sc. Ch 1, turn. 17 5-dc shells plus 2 3-dc shells.
Row 3 Sc in 1st dc, *5 dc in next sc, sk 2 dc, sc in next dc. Rep from * to end, placing last sc in top of t-ch. Ch 3, turn.
Rep Rows 2–3 for pattern until 35 rows have been completed, or Front measures desired width. End off.

Center Back
Orient one Front so that you are crocheting across a short side, with the foundation chain toward the hand you stitch with. The opposite long side will be the last row stitched.

WEDGE ONE
Row 1 (RS) Work 55 sc evenly spaced across the short edge of Front. Ch 1, turn.
Row 2 Sc in each sc across. Ch 1, turn.
Row 3 Sc across until 5 sts remain. Ch 1, turn. 50 sc.
Row 4 Sl st in 1st sc, sc in each sc across. Ch 1, turn.
Rep Rows 3–4 for pattern until the final repeat

continued on page 104

completed has only 5 sc. Number of scs in odd-numbered rows will decrease by 5 with every repeat.

WEDGE TWO

Row 1 Sc in each sc and sl st across. 55 sc.
Rep instructions for Wedge One, beginning with Row 2. Work as many wedges as desired—the sample shown has 5 wedges—and finish with a Row 1 of Wedge Two. End off, leaving a long tail for sewing.

Assembly

Work 55 sc evenly spaced across the short side of second Front. End off.

Line up the Fronts so that the sc row is opposite the final row of Center Back, and the foundation chain of one Front is on the same side of the wrap as the foundation chain of the other. Whip st the second Front to Center Back.

Work Wedge One on the remaining short side of each Front, orienting the work so that the widest part of the edge is toward the outside of the wrap. Do not end off. Ch 1, turn.

Edging

Rnd 1 Sc in each sc and sl st across the end of wedge just completed, 3 sc in corner, work across inner edge of Front, placing 2 sc in each ch-2 sp and 1 sc in the base of each shell or sc. Work sc evenly spaced across the narrow edge of Center Back section, work across the inner edge of 2nd Front, placing 2 sc in each ch-2 sp and 1 sc in the base of each shell or sc. Next, 3 sc in corner, sc in each sc and sl st across end of the other wedge, 2 sc in corner, work in pattern across the outer edge of Front (5 dc in each sc, sc in center dc of each 5-dc shell), sc evenly spaced around the outer edge of Center Back, then work in pattern across the outer edge of second Front, 3 sc in corner. Join rnd with sl st in 1st sc.

Rnd 2 Ch 1, do not turn, sc in each sc around, placing 3 sc in each corner, and working in pattern st along the outer edges of each Front. Join rnd with sl st in 1st sc. End off.

Weave in ends.

Block assembled wrap.

Stratum Wrap Schematic

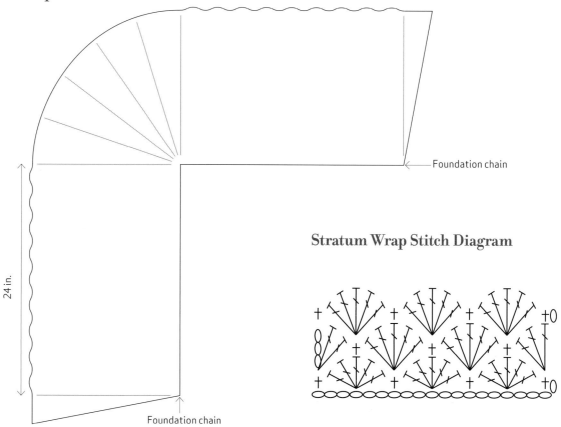

24 in.

Foundation chain

Foundation chain

Stratum Wrap Stitch Diagram

The wedges crocheted at the center back determine the angle at which the ends of the wrap cross in front. To increase or decrease the angle, just add or subtract single-crochet wedges. I prefer an odd number of wedges, but any number will work.

Banded Cowl

Thick, soft cowls are the perfect cure for the winter weather blahs, and this multihued wonder is sure to brighten your day. Plus, this one is stitched flat, then fastens with buttons, so you can put it on without messing up your hair! Button up some or all, for different looks as well as temperature control.

Tip: Quickly shape up this cowl by switching your hook sizes in sequence as you crochet. It's an easy technique that is often used in garments—you can create shaping while keeping to the stitch pattern, no math required.

SKILL LEVEL
Easy

FINISHED SIZE
27 in. wide at top edge, 45 in. wide at bottom edge, 23 in. long *before edging*

YARN
Lion Brand Yarn Amazing®; 5 skeins Arcadia, #825-206 (1.75 oz/147 yds); 735 yards worsted weight yarn (CYCA 4, Medium, see p. 146)

NOTIONS
Hook sizes I/9 U.S. (5.5 mm), J/10 U.S. (6 mm), K/10½ U.S. (6.5 mm), L/11 U.S. (8 mm), M/N-13 U.S. (9 mm), N/P-15 U.S. (10 mm)
10 or any even number of buttons, 1⅜ in. in diameter
Sewing needle and thread to match the buttons

GAUGE
Gauge not critical for this pattern. Pattern gauge changes every 6 rows.

NOTE
Ch-4 counts as 1 dc plus ch-1 throughout.

SPECIAL STITCHES
Dc3tog, a decrease: (Yo, insert hook in next st, yo, draw through st, yo, draw through 2 loops on hook) 3 times, yo, draw through all loops on hook.

Cowl
With largest hook, ch 109.
Set-Up Row Sc in 2nd ch from hook and in each of next 20 ch, *ch 3, sk 3 ch, sc in each of next 19 sc. Rep from * until 2 ch remain, sc in each of last 2 ch. Ch 4, turn. 99 sc.
Row 1 Dc in each of next 9 sc, dc3tog, dc in each of next 8 sc, *(dc, ch 3, dc) in ch-3 sp, dc in each of next 8 sc, dc3tog, dc in each of next 8 sc. Rep from * to last 2 sc, dc in next sc, ch 1, dc in last sc. Ch 4, turn.
Row 2 Dc in ch-1 sp, (ch 1, sk 1 dc, dc in next dc) 4 times, (sk 1 dc, dc in next dc) 2 times, (ch 1, sk 1 dc, dc in next dc) 3 times, ch 1, *(dc, ch 3, dc) in ch-3 sp, (ch 1, sk 1 dc, dc in next dc) 4 times, (sk 1 dc, dc in next dc) 2 times, (ch 1, sk 1 dc, dc in next dc) 3 times. Rep from * to last 2 sts, ch 1, (dc, ch 1, dc) in ch-1 sp. Ch 4, turn.
Row 3 (Dc in next ch-1 sp, dc in next dc) 4 times, dc in next ch-1 sp, dc3tog, (dc in next ch-1 sp, dc in next dc) 4 times, *(dc, ch 3, dc) in ch-3 sp, (dc in next dc, dc in next ch-1 sp) 4 times, dc3tog, (dc in next ch-1 sp, dc in next dc) 4 times. Rep from * to last ch-1 sp, (dc, ch 1, dc) in last ch-1 sp. Ch 1, turn.
Row 4 Sc in 1st dc, sc in ch-1 sp, sc in each of next 19 dc, *ch 3, sk ch-3 sp, sc in each of next 19 sc. Rep from * to last ch-1 sp, sc in last ch-1 sp, sc in last dc. Ch 4, turn.
Row 5 Dc in ch-1 sp, (ch 1, sk 1 sc, dc in next sc) 4 times, (sk 1 sc, dc in next sc) 2 times, (ch 1, sk 1 sc, dc in next

continued on page 109

Using button "cuff links" means you can roll the top down on the cowl and still see cute buttons rather than messy stitching where you would have sewed on a button.

sc) 3 times, ch 1, *(dc, ch 3, dc) in ch-3 sp, (ch 1, sk 1 sc, dc in next sc) 4 times, (sk 1 sc, dc in next sc) 2 times, (ch 1, sk 1 sc, dc in next sc) 3 times. Rep from * to last 3 sts, ch 1, sk 2 sc, dc in next sc, ch 1, dc in last sc. Ch 4, turn.

Row 6 Rep Row 3.

Row 7 Rep Row 2, ch 1, turn.

Row 8 *Sc in each dc and ch-1 sp across to ch-3 sp, ch 3, sk ch-3 sp. Rep from * across, sc in each dc and ch-1 sp to end. Ch 3, turn.

Rep Rows 1–8 until 37 total rows have been completed, stepping down one hook size after every 6th row. End off.

Side Edging (Each Side)

Row 1 With hook size J/10 U.S. (6 mm), work an odd number of sc sts up the side. Ch 1, turn.

Row 2 Sc in each sc across. Ch 3, turn.

Row 3 Dc in next sc, *ch 1, sk 1 sc, dc in next sc. Rep from * to end, dc in last sc. Ch 1, turn.

Row 4 Sc in each sc and ch-1 sp across. Ch 1, turn.

Row 5 Sc in each sc across. End off.

Finishing

Weave in all ends, block lightly.

Using sewing thread or extra yarn, stitch pairs of buttons back to back to form cuff links. Place as many or as few cuff links as you like through both sides of front edging to keep the cowl in place.

Banded Cowl Schematic

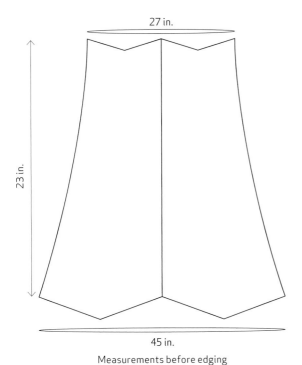

27 in.

23 in.

45 in.

Measurements before edging

Banded Cowl Stitch Diagram

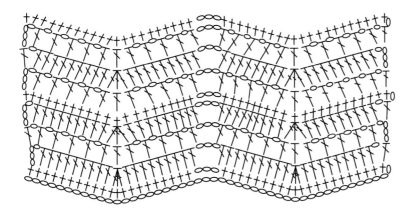

Coalesce Wrap

Small motifs join together to make a curved, crescent-shaped wrap that settles naturally around the neck. Because each motif is joined as you go, you can easily customize this pattern to make almost any shape wrap without adding to the time spent doing the finishing. Follow the diagram as shown, add motifs to the front panels to square off the look, or add motifs all around to make wraps of myriad shapes and sizes—from circular capelets to rectangular shawls.

DESIGNED BY CHARLES VOTH

Tip: Join-as-you-go stitching means you will attach each motif to its neighbors on the last round of stitching. This technique cuts way down on the amount of finishing you have to do when the crocheting is through.

SKILL LEVEL
Intermediate

FINISHED SIZE
42 x 45 in. *at the widest/longest point, after blocking*

YARN
Lorna's Laces Shepherd Sport; 6 skeins Fiddlehead (2.6 oz/200 yds); 1,200 yds DK weight yarn (CYCA 3, Light, see p. 146)

NOTIONS
Hook size G/6 U.S. (4 mm) *or size needed to obtain gauge*
Tapestry needle

GAUGE
Blocked motif is 3½ in. point to point and 3⅛ in. side to side.

NOTES
Ch-6 equals 1 tr plus ch-2 throughout.
Motifs are joined as you crochet the final rnd of the 2nd

and subsequent motifs by slip stitching into the center st of the ch-7 and ch-3 spaces from the final rnd of previously completed motifs. The hook should be inserted into the front loop of the center st to make the sl st join.

Motif

Rnd 1 *Ch 4, working in back of ch, sc in 2nd ch from hook, hdc in next ch, dc in next ch. Rep from * 3 times, sl st in 1st ch to join rnd. This forms 3 "petals."
Rnd 2 Ch 6 (equals 1 tr plus 2 ch), tr in ring in center of Rnd 1, *ch 4, sk 3 sts, sc in ch at tip of petal, ch 4, (tr, ch 2, tr) in center ring, rep from * 2 times, ch 4, sk 3 sts, sc in ch at tip of petal, ch 4, sl st 4th ch of beg ch-6.
Rnd 3 *Ch 7, sk 2, sl st in top of tr, (sc, hdc, ch 3, hdc, sc) in ch-4 sp, ch 7, (sc, hdc, ch3, hdc, sc) into next ch-4 sp, sl st in top of next tr st. Rep from * 3 times; sl st to final sl st of prev rnd.
End off.
To join subsequent motifs, work Rnds 1 and 2 as before. Work Rnd 3 as follows: Hold motif being crocheted with its WS against the adjacent motif, lining up the corresponding sides and points of the hexagon.
Joining Rnd 3 (joining 1 side): Ch 3, sl st join into front loop of the center st of the corresponding ch-7 loop on completed motif, ch 3, sk 2 sts, sl st in top of tr st, (sc, hdc, ch 1 sl st to join center st of ch-3 sp on corresponding

continued on page 113

Once you have the ends overlapped, you can arrange the whole wrap so it closes in the front or on either shoulder. Consider adding a shawl pin or brooch to keep it in place.

side of adjacent motif, ch 1, hdc, sc) in ch-4 sp, ch 3, sl st to join in center st of ch-7 loop on adjacent motif, ch 3, (sc, hdc, ch3, hdc, sc) into next ch-4 sp, sl st in top of next tr; *ch 7, sk 2 sts, sl st in top of tr, (sc, hdc, ch3, hdc, sc) in ch-4 sp, ch 7, (sc, hdc, ch 3, hdc, sc) into next ch-4 sp, sl st in top of next tr; rep from * 2 times; sl st to final sl st of prev rnd.

To join motifs on 2 or 3 sides, use the same technique in the ch-7 and ch-3 loops as above on as many sides as needed.

Shaping the Wrap

Work 3 motifs, joining into a row. Refer to the Coalesce Wrap Assembly Diagram for the placement of motifs 4–39.

Beginning a new section of the wrap, motifs 40–42 are worked in a row like motifs 1–3. Refer back to the assembly diagram for placement of motifs 43–78.

Refer to the assembly diagram for placement of motifs 79–116, which form the back and join the 2 fronts of the wrap.

Weave in all ends.

Block the assembled wrap.

Coalesce Wrap Motif Stitch Diagram

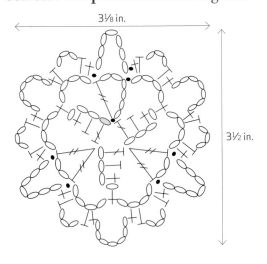

3⅛ in.

3½ in.

Coalesce Wrap Motif Joining Diagram

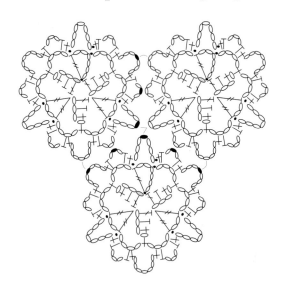

Coalesce Wrap Assembly Diagram

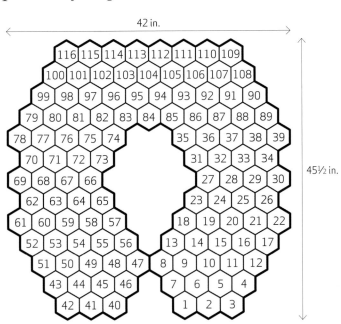

42 in.

45½ in.

Sensible Shawl

This shawl will quickly become one of the most versatile pieces in your wardrobe. I use mine in all sorts of ways, whether tied up or pinned as a shawl when indoors, or wrapped around my neck multiple times for a soft, squishy neckwarmer. The more layers you wear, the warmer it will be.

Tip: To make the shawl narrower at the bottom edge, work fewer chains in a multiple of 16—8 fewer chains/1 fewer stitch repeat on both sides of the central 7-dc shell. Just remember you will have to work additional rows of height to get the width you want at the top edge.

SKILL LEVEL
Easy

FINISHED SIZE
One size: 120 in. wide at top edge, 32 in. wide at bottom edge, 26 in. long *after blocking*

YARN
Plymouth Yarn® Company Zino; 2 skeins #08 (3.5 oz/ 436 yds); 872 yds fingering weight yarn (CYCA 2, Fine, see p. 146)

NOTIONS
Hook size H/8 U.S. (5 mm)
Stitch marker
Tapestry needle

GAUGE
10 rows and 16 sts = 4 in. in patt st *slightly stretched but not blocked. Gauge not critical for this pattern.*

NOTES
Ch-3 counts as 1 dc throughout.
Ch-4 counts as 1 tr throughout.

Shawl

Ch 154.

Row 1 Sc in 2nd ch from hook, (sk 3 ch, 4 dc in next ch, ch 3, sk 3 ch, sc in next ch) 9 times, sk 3 ch, 7 dc in next ch, placing marker in 3rd dc of 7, sk 3 ch, sc in next ch, (ch 3, sk 3 ch, 4 dc in next ch, sk 3 ch, sc in next ch) 9 times. Ch 4, turn. 19 shells.

Row 2 Tr in 1st sc, ch 5, sk 3 dc, sc in next dc, *ch 7, sk 3 dc, sc in next dc. Rep from * until sc is made in marked st, mark this sc, **ch 7, sk ch-3 sp, sc in next dc. Rep from ** to end, ch 5, 2 tr in last sc. Ch 3, turn.

Row 3 3 dc in 1st tr, ch 3, sc in ch-5 sp, *4 dc in next sc, ch 3, sc in next ch-7 sp. Rep from * to marked st, 7 dc in marked st, placing marker in 3rd dc of 7, sc in next ch-7 sp, **ch 3, 4 dc in next sc, sc in next ch-7 sp. Rep from ** to end, ch 3, sk 1 tr, 4 dc in last dc. Ch 4, turn. 21 shells.

Row 4 Tr in 1st dc, ch 5, sk 3 dc, sc in next dc, *ch 7, sk 3 dc, sc in next dc. Rep from * until sc is made in marked st, mark this sc, **ch 7, sk ch-3 sp, sc in next dc. Rep from ** to end, ch 5, sk 2 dc, 2 tr in last dc. Ch 3, turn. Rep Rows 3 and 4 for pattern until work measures 26 in. or desired height at center back, ending with a Row 4. Do not end off after final row, ch 1, turn. There will be 2 more shells after every repeat.

Edging

Rnd 1 [top] Sc across top of shawl, placing 7 sc in each ch-7 sp and 1 sc in each sc to end, in each tr and ch-1 sp,

continued on page 116

ch 4, [side] working along side of shawl, 3 tr in side/top of tr, *sl st in same st as base of next shell, ch 4, 3 tr in same sp, sl st in top/side of next tr, 3 tr in same sp. Rep from * to end of side, [corner] sl st in corner st, ch 4, 5 tr in same st, ch 4, sl st in same st, [bottom] ch 4, 3 tr in same st, **sk ch-3 sp, sl st in base of next shell, ch 4, 3 tr in same st. Rep from ** 7 more times (you will be at the center of the bottom edge), ***sk ch-3 sp, 3 tr in base of next shell, ch 4, sl st in same st. Rep from *** to end of bottom edge [corner], ch 4, 5 tr in same st, ch 4, sl st in same st, [side] ****3 tr in side/top of next tr, ch 4, sl st in same st, 3 tr in base next shell, ch 4, sl st in same st. Rep from **** to end, placing last group of sts in top point of shawl. [top] Sc in each sc across top of shawl to end of top edge. End off.
Weave in ends; block.

Sensible Shawl Stitch Diagram

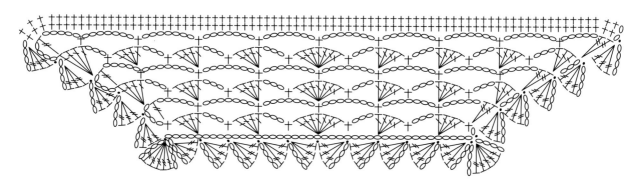

This sample is shown in a yarn with a long color repeat, giving it a striped appearance. The pattern also would work well in a solid or multicolored yarn.

Wrapt Top

Use this close-fitting, lacy top to add a quick dash of color to an otherwise plain outfit. The lace stitch repeats are placed in such a way that there is additional fabric in the front of the sweater to accommodate the bustline without having to do short-row shaping.

Tip: Single-crochet seams are best on lace patterns. While they add too much bulk to denser fabrics, they keep a lace piece looking good both inside and out by adding a little structure and cover-up to any uneven edges.

SKILL LEVEL
Intermediate

FINISHED SIZE
Underbust Band: L (XL, 2X, 3X, 4X, 5X); 44 (48, 52, 56, 60, 64) in. *Band crosses in front during wear.*

YARN
Rowan® Panama; 5 (6, 6, 7, 8, 8) skeins Dahlia, #305 (50 g/148 yds); 740 (888, 888, 1,036, 1,184, 1,184) yds DK weight yarn (CYCA 3, Light, see p. 146)

NOTIONS
Hook size G/6 U.S. (4 mm) *or size needed to obtain gauge*

GAUGE
4 ch-5 sps and 8 rows = 4 in. in Sleeve patt st

Underbust Band

Ch 8.
Row 1 Sc in 2nd ch from hook and in each ch across. Ch 1, turn. 7 sc.
Row 2 Sctbl in each sc across. Ch 1, turn.
Rep Row 2 for pattern until work measures 44 (48, 52, 56, 60, 64) in. from beg. Do not end off, ch 1, turn work 90 degrees to work along adjacent long side.

Body

Row 1 Work 167 (190, 213, 236, 259, 282) sc evenly spaced along the upper edge of Underbust Band. Ch 1, turn.
Rows 2–3 Sc in each sc across. Ch 1, turn.
Row 4 Sc in 1st sc, (ch 5, sk 3 sc, sc in next sc) 4 times, (ch 5, sk 2 sc, sc in next sc) 12 (14, 16, 18, 20, 22) times, (ch 5, sk 3 sc, sc in next sc, ch 5, sk 2 sc, sc in next sc) 10 (11, 12, 13, 14, 15) times, (ch 5, sk 2 sc, sc in next sc) 12 (14, 16, 18, 20 22) times, (ch 5, sk 3 sc, sc in next sc) 4 times. Ch 5, turn. 52 (58, 64, 70, 76, 84) ch-5 sps.
Row 5 Sc in 1st ch-5 sp, 5 dc in next sc, sc in next ch-5 sp, *ch 5, sc in next ch-5 sp, 5 dc in next sc, sc in next ch-5 sp. Rep from * to end, ch 2, dc in last sc. Ch 1, turn.
Row 6 Sl st in 1st dc, ch 2, sk 2 dc, sc in next dc, *ch 5, sc in next ch-5 sp, ch 5, sk 2 dc, sc in next dc. Rep from * to end, ch 2, sk 2 dc, sc in last sc. Ch 1, turn. 50 (56, 62, 68, 74, 82) ch-5 sps plus 2 ch-2 sps.
Row 7 Sl st in 1st sc, sl st in each ch of ch-2 sp, sl st in next sc, ch 2, sc in next ch-5 sp, 5 dc in next sc, sc in next ch-5 sp, *ch 5, sc in next ch-5 sp, 5 dc in next sc, sc in next ch-5 sp. Rep from * to end, leave last ch-2 sp unworked. Ch 1, turn. 25 (28, 31, 34, 37, 40) 5-dc shells plus 24 (27, 30, 31, 32, 39) ch-5 sps.
Row 8 Sl st in 1st sc and in each of 1st 2 dc, sc in next dc, *ch 5, sc in next ch-5 sp, ch 5, sk 2 dc, sc in next dc. Rep from * to end. Ch 1, turn. 48 (54, 60, 66, 74, 80) ch-5 sps.
Row 9 Sl st in 1st sc, sl st in each of 1st 2 ch of ch-5 sp, sc in same ch-5 sp, 5 dc in next sc, sc in next ch-5 sp, *ch 5, sc in next ch-5 sp, 5 dc in next sc, sc in next ch-5 sp. Rep from * to end. Ch 1, turn. 24 (27, 30, 33, 37, 40) ch-5 shells plus 23 (26, 29, 32, 35, 38) ch-5 sps.

continued on page 120

Rows 10–13 (15, 15, 17, 17, 17) Rep Rows 8–9 2 (3, 3, 4, 4, 4) times. 44 (48, 54, 58, 66, 72) ch-5 sps.

Divide Fronts and Back

RIGHT FRONT

Row 1 Sl st in 1st sc and in each of 1st 2 dc, sc in next dc, *ch 5, sc in next ch-5 sp, ch 5, sk 2 dc, sc in next dc. Rep from * 4 (4, 5, 6, 7, 8) times, ch 5, sc in next ch-5 sp. Ch 1, turn. 11 (11, 13, 15, 19, 21) ch-5 sps.

Row 2 Sl st in 1st sc and in each of 1st 2 ch, sc in same ch-5 sp, *ch 5, sc in next ch-5 sp, 5 dc in next sc, sc in next ch-5 sp. Rep from * to end. Ch 1, turn. 5 (5, 6, 7, 9, 10) ch-5 shells plus 5 (5, 6, 7, 9, 10) ch-5 sps.

Row 3 Sl st in 1st sc and in each of 1st 2 dc, sc in next dc, *ch 5, sc in next ch-5 sp, ch 5, sk 2 dc, sc in next dc. Rep from * 3 (3, 4, 5, 7, 8) times, ch 5, sc in next ch-5 sp. Ch 1, turn. 9 (9, 11, 13, 17, 19) ch-5 sps.

Row 4 Rep Row 2. 4 (4, 5, 6, 8, 9) ch-5 shells plus 4 (4, 5, 6, 8, 9) ch-5 sps.

Row 5 Sl st in 1st sc and in each of 1st 2 dc, sc in next dc, *ch 5, sc in next ch-5 sp, ch 5, sk 2 dc, sc in next dc. Rep from * 2 (2, 3, 4, 6, 7) times, ch 5, sc in next ch-5 sp, ch 2, dc in last sc. Ch 3, turn. 7 (7, 9, 11, 15, 17) ch-5 sps.

Row 6 2 dc in 1st dc, sc in next ch-5 sp, *ch 5, sc in next ch-5 sp, 5 dc in next sc, sc in next ch-5 sp. Rep from * to end. Ch 1, turn. 3 (3, 4, 5, 7, 8) ch-5 shells plus 3 (3, 4, 5, 7, 8) ch-5 sps.

Row 7 Sl st in 1st sc and in each of 1st 2 dc, sc in next dc, *ch 5, sc in next ch-5 sp, ch 5, sk 2 dc, sc in next dc. Rep from * to end, placing last sc in top of t-ch. Ch 5, turn. 6 (6, 8, 10, 14, 18) ch-5 sps.

Row 8 Sc in 1st ch-5 sp, 5 dc in next sc, sc in next ch-5 sp, *ch 5, sc in next ch-5 sp, 5 dc in next sc, sc in next ch-5 sp. Rep from * to end. Ch 1, turn. 3 (3, 4, 5, 7, 8) 5-dc shells plus 2 (2, 3, 4, 6, 7) ch-5 sps plus 1 ch-2 sp.

Row 9 Sl st in 1st sc and in each of 1st 2 dc, sc in next dc, *ch 5, sc in next ch-5 sp, ch 5, sk 2 dc, sc in next dc. Rep from * to end, ch 5, sc in sp created by t-ch. Ch 3, turn. 6 (6, 7, 8, 10, 11) ch-5 sps.

Rows 10–12 Rep Rows 6–8. Sizes L and XL only, ch 5, turn, skip to Row 21. 2 (2, 3, 4, 6, 7) 5-dc shells plus 1 (1, 2, 3, 5, 6) ch-5 sp(s) plus ch-2 sp.

Sizes 2X (3X, 4X, 5X) only:

Rows 13–16 Rep Row 9, then Rows 6–8. Sizes 2X and 3X only, ch 5, turn, skip to Row 21. 2 (3, 5, 6) 5-dc shells plus 1 (2, 4, 5) ch-5 sp(s) plus ch-2 sp.

Sizes 4X (5X) only:

Rows 17–20 Rep Row 9, then Rows 6–8. Ch 5, turn after

Row 8. 4 (5) 5-dc shells plus 3 (4) ch-5 sps plus ch-2 sp.

All sizes:

Row 21 Sk 2 dc, sc in next dc, ch 5, sc in next ch-5 sp, ch 5, sk 2 dc, sc in next dc, ch 5, sc in top of t-ch. Ch 3, turn.

Row 22 2 dc in 1st sc, sc in next ch-5 sp, ch 5, sc in next ch-5 sp, 5 dc in next sc, sc in next ch-5 sp, ch 5, sc in sp created by t-ch. Ch 5, turn. 1½ shells, 2 ch-5 sps.

Row 23 Sc in 1st 5 ch-5 sp, ch 5, sk 2 dc, sc in next dc, ch 5, sc in next ch-5 sp, ch 5, sc in top of t-ch. Ch 5, turn.

Row 24 Sc in 1st ch-5 sp, 5 dc in next sc, sc in next ch-5 sp, ch 5, sc in next ch-5 sp, 3 dc in sp created by t-ch. Ch 1, turn. 1½ shells, 1 ch-5 sp, 1 ch-2 sp. Ch 1, turn.

Row 25 Sc in 1st dc, ch 5, sc in next ch-5 sp, ch 5, sk 2 dc, sc in next dc, ch 5, sc in space created by t-ch. End off.

BACK

Row 1 Working in the same direction as Row 1 of Right Front, skip 5-dc shell, sc in next ch-5 sp, *ch 5, sk 2 dc, sc in next dc, ch 5, sc in next ch-5 sp. Rep from * 7 (9, 10, 10, 10, 11) times. Ch 1, turn. 16 (20, 22, 22, 22, 24) ch-5 sps.

Row 2 Sl st in 1st sc and in each of 1st 2 ch, sc in same ch-5 sp, *ch 5, sc in next ch-5 sp, 5 dc in next sc, sc in next ch-5 sp. Rep from * to end, ch 5, sc in next ch-5 sp. Ch 1, turn. 7 (9, 10, 10, 10, 11) ch-5 shells plus 8 (9, 11, 11, 11, 12) ch-5 sps.

Row 3 Sl st in 1st sc and in each of 1st 2 ch, sc in same ch-5 sp, *ch 5, sk 2 dc, sc in next dc, ch 5, sc in next ch-5 sp. Rep from * to end. Ch 1, turn. 14 (18, 20, 20, 20, 22) ch-5 sps.

Row 4 Rep Row 2, ch 5, turn. 6 (8, 9, 9, 9, 10) ch-5 shells plus 7 (9, 10, 10, 10, 11) ch-5 sps.

Row 5 Sc in 1st ch-5 sp, * ch 5, sk 2 dc, sc in next dc, ch 5, sc in next ch-5 sp. Rep from * to end, ch 2, dc in last sc. Ch 3, turn. 12 (16, 18, 18, 18, 20) ch-5 sps.

Row 6 2 dc in 1st dc, sc in next ch-5 sp, ch 5, sc in next ch-5 sp, *5 dc in next sc, sc in next ch-5 sp, ch 5, sc in next ch-5 sp. Rep from * to end, 3 dc in sp created by t-ch. Ch 1, turn. 5 (7, 8, 8, 8, 9) ch-5 shells plus 6 (8, 9, 9, 9, 10) ch-5 sps plus 2 3-dc shells.

Row 7 Sc in 1st dc, *ch 5, sc in next ch-5 sp, ch 5, sk 2 dc, sc in next dc. Rep from * to end, placing last sc in top of t-ch. Ch 5, turn. 14 (16, 18, 18, 18, 20) ch-5 sps.

Row 8 Sc in 1st ch-5 sp, 5 dc in next sc, sc in next ch-5 sp, *ch 5, sc in next ch-5 sp, 5 dc in next sc, sc in next ch-5 sp. Rep from * to end, ch 2, dc in last sc. Ch 1, turn. 6 (8, 9, 9, 9, 10) 5-dc shells plus 5 (7, 8, 8, 8, 9) ch-5 sps, plus 2 ch-2 sps.

Row 9 Sc in 1st dc, ch 5, sk 2 dc, sc in next dc, *ch 5, sc in next ch-5 sp, ch 5, sk 2 dc, sc in next dc. Rep from * to end, ch 5, sc in sp created by t-ch. Ch 3, turn. 12 (16, 18, 18, 18, 20) ch-5 sps.

Row 10 Rep Row 6, placing final 3 dc in last sc.

Rows 11–13 Rep Rows 7–9.

Rows 14–20 Rep Rows 10–13, then Rows 10–12.

Row 21 Sc in 1st dc, ch 5, sk 2 dc, sc in next dc, ch 5, sc in next ch-5 sp, ch 5, sk 2 dc, sc in next dc. End off, sk 5 5-dc shells, sc in center dc in next 5-dc shell, ch 5, sc in next ch-5 sp, ch 5, sk 2 dc, sc in next dc, ch 5, sc in sp created by t-ch. End off.

LEFT FRONT

Row 1 Working in the same direction as Row 1 of Right Front, sk 5-dc shell, sc in next ch-5 sp, ch 5, sk 2 dc, sc in next dc, *ch 5, sc in next ch-5 sp, ch 5, sk 2 dc, sc in next dc. Rep from * to end. Ch 1, turn. 11 (11, 13, 15, 19, 21) ch-5 sps.

Row 2 Sl st in 1st sc and in each of 1st 2 ch, sc in same ch-5 sp, *5 dc in next sc, sc in next ch-5 sp, ch 5, sc in next ch-5 sp. Rep from * to end. Ch 1, turn. 5 (5, 6, 7, 9, 10) ch-5 shells plus 5 (5, 6, 7, 9, 10) ch-5 sps.

Row 3 Sl st in 1st sc and in each of 1st 2 ch, sc in same ch-5 sp, ch 5, sk 2 dc, sc in next dc, *ch 5, sc in next ch-5 sp, ch 5, sk 2 dc, sc in next sc. Rep from * to end. Ch 1, turn. 9 (9, 11, 13, 17, 19) ch-5 sps.

Row 4 Rep Row 2. Ch 5, turn. 4 (4, 5, 6, 8, 9) ch-5 shells plus 4 (4, 5, 6, 8, 9) ch-5 sps.

Row 5 Sc in 1st ch-5 sp, ch 5, sk 2 dc, sc in next dc, *ch 5, sc in next ch-5 sp, ch 5, sk 2 dc, sc in next dc. Rep from * to end. Ch 1, turn. 7 (7, 9, 11, 15, 17) ch-5 sps.

Row 6 Sl st in 1st sc and in each of 1st 2 ch, sc in same ch-5 sp *5 dc in next sc, sc in next ch-5 sp, ch 5, sc in next ch-5 sp. Rep from * to end, 3 dc in sp created by t-ch. Ch 1, turn. 3 (3, 4, 5, 7, 8) ch-5 shells plus 3 (3, 4, 5, 7, 8) ch-5 sps.

Row 7 Sc in 1st dc, *ch 5, sc in next ch-5 sp, ch 5, sk 2 dc, sc in next dc. Rep from * to end. Ch 1, turn. 6 (6, 8, 10, 14, 18) ch-5 sps.

Row 8 Sl st in 1st sc and in each of 1st 2 ch, sc in same ch-5 sp, 5 dc in next sc, sc in next ch-5 sp, *ch 5, sc in next ch-5 sp, 5 dc in next sc, sc in next ch-5 sp. Rep from * to end, ch 2, dc in last sc. Ch 1, turn. 3 (3, 4, 5, 7, 8) 5-dc shells plus 2 (2, 3, 4, 6, 7) ch-5 sps plus 1 ch-2 sp.

Row 9 Sc in 1st dc, *ch 5, sk 2 dc, sc in next dc, ch 5, sc in next ch-5 sp. Rep from * to end. Ch 1, turn. 6 (6, 7, 8, 10, 11) ch-5 sps.

Rows 10–12 Rep Rows 6–8. Sizes L and XL, ch 5, turn, sk to Row 21. 2 (2, 3, 4, 6, 7) 5-dc shells + 1 (1, 2, 3, 5, 6) ch-5 sp(s) + ch-2 sp.

Sizes 2X (3X, 4X, 5X) only:

Rows 13–16 Rep Row 9, then Rows 6–8. Sizes 2X and 3X only, ch 5, turn, skip to Row 21. 2 (3, 5, 6) 5-dc shells plus 1 (2, 4, 5) ch-5 sp(s) plus ch-2 sp.

Sizes 4X (5X) only:

Rows 17–20 Rep Row 9, then Rows 6–8. Ch 5, turn after Row 8. 4 (5) 5-dc shells plus 3 (4) ch-5 sps plus ch-2 sp.

All sizes:

Row 21 Sc in 1st dc, ch 5, sk 2 dc, sc in next dc, ch 5, sc in next ch-5 sp, ch 5, sk 2 dc, sc in next dc. End off.

Sleeves (Make 2)

BAND

Rep instructions for Underbust Band until work measures 12 (12, 12, 14, 14, 16) in. from beg. Do not end off, ch 1, turn work 90 degrees to work along adjacent long side.

SLEEVE PROPER

Row 1 Work 49 (49, 49, 57, 57, 65) sc evenly spaced along upper edge of Sleeve Band. Ch 1, turn.

Rows 2–3 Sc in each sc across. Ch 1, turn.

Row 4 Sc in 1st sc, *ch 5, sk 3 sc, sc in next sc. Rep from * to end. Ch 5, turn. 12 (12, 12, 14, 14, 16) ch-5 sps.

Row 5 Sc in 1st ch-5 sp, 5 dc in next sc, sc in next ch-5 sp, *ch 5, sc in next ch-5 sp, 5 dc in next sc, sc in next ch-5 sp. Rep from * to end, ch 2, dc in last sc. Ch 1, turn. 6 (6, 6, 7, 7, 8) 5-dc shells, 5 (5, 5, 6, 6, 7) ch-5 sps plus 2 ch-2 sps.

Row 6 Sc in 1st dc, *ch 5, sk 2 dc, sc in next dc, ch 5, sc in next ch-5 sp. Rep from * to end, placing last sc in 3rd ch of t-ch. Ch 3, turn.

Row 7 4 dc in 1st sc, sc in next ch-5 sp, ch 5, sc in next ch-5 sp, *5 dc in next sc, sc in next ch-5 sp, ch 5, sc in next ch-5 sp. Rep from * to end, 5 dc in last sc. Ch 5, turn. 6 (6, 6, 7, 7, 8) 5-dc shells, 5 (5, 5, 6, 6, 7) ch-5 sps plus 2 ch-2 sps plus 2 4-dc shells.

Row 8 Sk 2 dc, sc in next dc, *ch 5, sc in next ch-5 sp, ch 5, sk 2 dc, sc in next dc. Rep from * to end, ch 2, dc in last dc. Ch 1, turn. 12 (12, 12, 14, 14, 16) ch-5 sps plus 2 ch-2 sps.

Row 9 Sc in 1st dc, *ch 5, sc in next ch-5 sp, 5 dc in next sc, sc in next ch-5 sp. Rep from * to end, ch 5, sc in 3rd ch of t-ch. Ch 4, turn. 6 (6, 6, 7, 7, 8) 5-dc shells, 7 (7, 7, 8, 8, 9) ch-5 sps.

Row 10 Sc in 2nd ch from hook, ch 5, sc in next ch-5 sp, *ch 5, sk 2 dc, sc in next dc, ch 5, sc in next ch-5 sp. Rep from * to end, ch 5, dc in last sc. Ch 5, turn. 14 (14, 14, 16, 16, 18) ch-5 sps.

continued on page 122

Rows 11–16 Rep Rows 5–10. 16, (16, 16, 18, 18, 20) ch-5 sps.

Rows 17–21 Rep Rows 5–9, ch 1, turn after Row 21. 8 (8, 8, 9, 9, 10) 5-dc shells, 9 (9, 9, 10, 10, 11) ch-5 sps. Sizes L (XL, 2X), go to Sleeve Cap Shaping.

Sizes 3X (4X, 5X) only:
Rows 22–27 Rep Row 10, then Rows 5–9, ch 1, turn after Row 27. 10 (10, 11) 5-dc shells plus 11 (11, 12) ch-5 sps.

SLEEVE CAP SHAPING

Row 1 Sl st in 1st sc, sl st in each of 3 ch of ch-5 sp, ch 3, sk 2 dc, sl st in next dc, ch 3, sc in next ch-5 sp, *ch 5, sk 2 dc, sc in next dc, ch 5, sc in next ch-5 sp. Rep from * 5 (5, 5, 7, 7, 8) times. Ch 1, turn. 12 (12, 12, 16, 16, 18) ch-5 sps.

Row 2 Sl st in 1st sc and in each of 1st 2 ch, sc in same ch-5 sp, *ch 5, sc in next ch-5 sp, 5 dc in next sc, sc in next ch-5 sp. Rep from * to end, ch 5, sc in next ch-5 sp. Ch 1, turn. 5 (5, 5, 7, 7, 8) ch-5 shells plus 6 (6, 6, 8, 8, 9) ch-5 sps.

Wrapt Top is in a stretchy stitch pattern, and the fit is adjustable according to how it is tied. Use the underbust band measurement to choose the size you want to make.

Row 3 Sl st in 1st sc and in each of 1st 2 ch, sc in same ch-5 sp, *ch 5, sk 2 dc, sc in next dc, ch 5, sc in next ch-5 sp. Rep from * to end. Ch 1, turn. 10 (10, 10, 14, 14, 16) ch-5 sps.

Row 4 Rep Row 2, ch 5, turn. 4 (4, 4, 6, 6, 7) ch-5 shells plus 5 (5, 5, 7, 7, 8) ch-5 sps.

Row 5 Sc in 1st ch-5 sp, *ch 5, sk 2 dc, sc in next dc, ch 5, sc in next ch-5 sp. Rep from * to end, ch 2, dc in last sc. Ch 1, turn. 8 (8, 8, 12, 12, 14) ch-5 sps plus 2 ch-2 sps.

Row 6 Sc in 1st sc, 5 dc in next sc, sc in next ch-5 sp, *ch 5, sc in next ch-5 sp, 5 dc in next sc, sc in next ch-5 sp. Rep from * to end, placing last sc in 3rd ch of t-ch. Ch 5, turn. 5 (5, 5, 7, 7, 8) ch-5 shells plus 4 (4, 4, 6, 6, 7) ch-5 sps.

Row 7 Sk 2 dc, sc in next dc, *ch 5, sc in next ch-5 sp, ch 5, sk 2 dc, sc in next sc. Rep from * to end, ch 2, dc in last sc. Ch 1, turn. 8 (8, 8, 12, 12, 14) ch-5 sps plus 2 ch-2 sps.

Row 8 Sc in 1st dc, ch 5, sc in next ch-5 sp, *5 dc in next sc, sc in next ch-5 sp, ch 5, sc in next sc. Rep from * to end, placing last sc in 3rd ch of t-ch. Ch 1, turn. 4 (4, 4, 6, 6, 7) ch-5 shells plus 5 (5, 5, 7, 7, 8) ch-5 sps.

Rows 9–13 (13, 13, 15, 15, 15) Rep Rows 3–4 2 (2, 2, 3, 3, 3) times, then Row 3 once more. End off. 4 (4, 4, 4, 4, 6) ch-5 sps.

Assembly

Sew Fronts to Back at shoulders. Fold each Sleeve with RS facing, then seam together with 1 row of sc. Turn sleeves RS out and attach to Body with 1 rnd sc.

Neckline Edging

Row 1 With RS facing, beg at bottom edge of Front, sctbl of each of 7 sts of Underbust Band, sc evenly up one side of front neckline, across back neck edge, down the side of the other front neckline, and sctbl of each of 7 sts of Underbust Band.

Rows 2–3 Ch 1, sctbl of each of 1st 7 sts, sc in each sc across until 7 sts remain, sctbl of each sc to end. End off after Row 3.

Ties

Make one on each side of Front.
Row 1 Sctbl of each of 1st 7 sts on edge of Front. Ch 1, turn.
Row 2 Sctbl of each sc across. Ch 1, turn.
Rep Row 2 for pattern until tie measures 35 in. or desired length. End off.

Wrapt Top Schematics

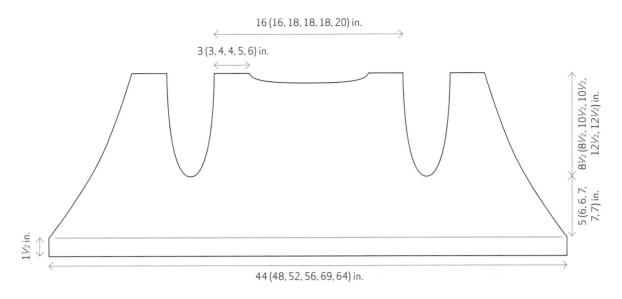

16 (16, 18, 18, 18, 20) in.

3 (3, 4, 4, 5, 6) in.

8½ (8½, 10½, 10½, 12½, 12½) in.

5 (6, 6, 7, 7, 7) in.

1½ in.

44 (48, 52, 56, 69, 64) in.

SLEEVE

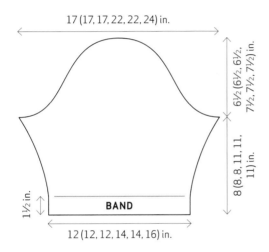

17 (17, 17, 22, 22, 24) in.

6½ (6½, 6½, 7½, 7½, 7½) in.

8 (8, 8, 11, 11, 11) in.

1½ in.

BAND

12 (12, 12, 14, 14, 16) in.

Wrapt Top Stitch Diagram

Shimmer Scarf

We all succumb to impulse buys at the yarn shop and wind up with a special skein of delicious fiber that we just couldn't resist! But what to do with just a single skein? Work up a quick, chic accessory, of course. This scarf is sure to add a splash of glamour to any outfit.

Tip: This scarf pattern makes the most of a skein of fancy yarn by working from the center out. Weigh the skein on a small kitchen scale before you begin, then work the pattern until exactly half the yarn has been used. You'll work the pattern from the center in the opposite direction with the remaining yarn. This way you know you will have enough yarn to complete the whole project.

SKILL LEVEL
Easy

FINISHED SIZE
One size: 6 x 80 in.

YARN
Tilli Tomas Disco Lights; 1 skein Hibiscus (90% spun silk/10% petite sequins); 225 yds fancy DK weight yarn (CYCA 3, Light, see p. 146)

NOTIONS
Hook size H/8 U.S. (5 mm) *or size needed to obtain gauge*

GAUGE
Gauge not critical for this pattern, just aim for a pleasing fabric.

SPECIAL STITCHES

Cl: Yo, insert hook in same ch-5 sp, yo, draw through st, yo, draw through 2 loops on hook, yo twice, insert hook in next st, yo, draw through st, (yo, draw through 2 loops on hook) twice, yo, insert hook in next ch-5 sp, yo, draw through st, yo, draw through 2 loops on hook, yo, draw through all 4 loops on hook.
Endcl: Used only at end of row. Yo, insert hook in same ch-5 sp, yo, draw through st, yo, draw through 2 loops on hook, yo twice, insert hook in top of t-ch, yo, draw through st, (yo, draw through 2 loops on hook) twice, yo, draw through all 3 loops on hook.
Sc3tog: (Insert hook in next st, yo, and bring up a loop) 3 times, yo, and pull through all 4 loops on hook.

First Half
Ch 18.
Row 1 Sc in 2nd ch from hook, *ch 5, sk 3 ch, sc in next ch. Rep from * to end. Ch 4, turn. 4 ch-5 loops.
Row 2 Dc in 1st ch-5 sp, *ch 5, cl. Rep from * to end, endcl. Ch 4, turn.
Rep Row 2 for pattern until scarf measures 38 in. from beg., or 5 in. less than one half of desired length.

FIRST POINT
Row 1 Dc in 1st ch-5 sp, *ch 4, cl. Rep from * to end, endcl. Ch 4, turn.
Row 2 Dc in 1st ch-5 sp, *ch 3, cl. Rep from * to end, endcl. Ch 4, turn.

continued on page 126

Row 3 Dc in 1st ch-5 sp, *ch 2, cl. Rep from * to end, endcl. Ch 4, turn.

Row 4 Dc in 1st ch-5 sp, *ch 1, cl. Rep from * to end, endcl. Ch 4, turn.

Row 5 Dc in 1st ch-5 sp, cl 3 times, endcl. Ch 4, turn.

Row 6 Dc2tog twice, dc in top of t-ch. Ch 1, turn.

Row 7 Sc3tog. End off.

Second Half

Row 1 Working in the opposite side of the foundation ch, attach yarn in 1st sc, ch 4, dc in next ch-3 sp, * ch 5, cl, placing 1st and last part of cl st in designated ch-3 sps. Rep from * to end, endcl placing 1st part of cluster st in last ch-3 sp. Ch 4, turn.

Rep instructions for First Half, beginning with Row 2. Block lightly, weave in all ends.

Shimmer Scarf Stitch Diagram

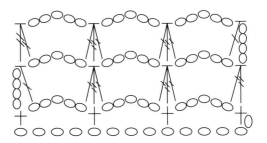

As a general rule: the fancier the yarn, the simpler the stitch pattern. Too much pattern can compete with glitz or color variations rather than complementing them.

Carryall

Fashion magazines love to tout the next "it" bag, and the next big thing often seems to be oversized. Some people say that toting a big bag makes your butt look smaller . . . I don't know whether that's true, but I do like to carry a bag in proportion to my frame. The crochet Carryall is felted for durability, and plastic canvas sheets, found at most craft stores, help to shape the sides and bottom of the bag. Customize yours using any range of eye-catching colors you like.

Tip: For this and every striped project, you get a neater edge if you make the final yarn over of the last stitch of the old color using the new color. Then make your turning chains in the new color, and carry on stitching.

SKILL LEVEL
Easy

FINISHED SIZE
One size: 15 x 4 x 12 in. *Felting is an art rather than a science; the finished measurements for each bag may vary.*

YARN
Brown Sheep Lamb's Pride Bulky; 6 skeins Onyx, #M-05 (Color A) and 1/3 skein/40 yds each of Wine Splash, #VM-235 (Color B); Sun Yellow, #M-13 (Color C); Red Hot Passion #M-197 (Color D); Deep Pine #M-172 (Color E); Orange You Glad, #M-110 (Color F); and Wild Mustard, #M-174 (Color G) (100 g/125 yds); 1,000 yds bulky weight yarn suitable for felting (CYCA 5, Bulky, see p. 146)

NOTIONS
Hook size N/13 U.S. (10 mm) or larger
Tapestry needle
Optional: 2 large sheets of plastic canvas for lining
Optional: Sewing needle and black thread

GAUGE
7 sts and 4 rows = 4 in. in dc. *Gauge not critical for this pattern.*

NOTES
Ch-3 counts as 1 dc throughout.
For felting instructions, see p. 129.

Bag Body

With Color A, ch 124.
Row 1 Dc in each 4th ch from hook and in each ch across. Ch 3, turn. 122 dc.
Row 2 Dc in each dc across. Ch 3, turn.
Row 3 Work 81 dc (counting t-ch as 1 dc), change to Color B, dc in each dc to end. Ch 3, turn.
Row 4 Work 41 dc in Color B, change to Color A, dc in each dc to end.
Row 5 Work 81 dc, change to Color B, dc in each dc to end, change to Color C, ch 3, turn.
Row 6 Work 41 dc in Color C, change to Color A, dc in each dc to end.
Row 7 Work 81 dc, change to Color C, dc in each dc to end.
Row 8 Rep Row 6.
Rep Rows 2–8 for pattern, always working the Color A sts in Color A, and changing the contrast color after every 3rd row.
When 3 rows have been completed with each of the 6 contrast colors, change to Color A and work 2 rows even. End off.

continued on page 129

Strap/Gusset

With Color A, ch 12.

Row 1 Dc in 4th ch from hook and in each ch across.
Ch 3, turn. 10 dc.

Work even in dc on these sts until work measures 90 in. from beg. End off.

Assembly

Fold the Bag Body so that the Color A section forms a U-shape, WSs facing each other. Pin the Strap/Gusset so that the multicolored flap is loose, and the short edge of the Color A side is parallel with the start of the color changes opposite. Attach the strap to the front, bottom, and back of the bag by working a row of sc on the RS of the bag. Attach the 2nd side of the strap to match. Weave in all ends.

Felt the assembled bag using the following felting instructions.

Optional: Measure the dimensions of the bottom and sides of your completed bag and cut sheets of plastic canvas to fit. Tack the plastic canvas into place using a sewing needle and thread.

Felting

To felt in a top-loading washing machine, put the completed item to be felted in a zipped mesh bag or a loosely knotted pillowcase. Place the bag in the washer with an old pair of jeans or two to provide additional agitation, and add a small amount of soap. Choose a small load size, the hottest water setting, and the highest agitation setting possible.

Check on the bag after 10 minutes and continue checking in 5-minute intervals, resetting the machine as needed. Do *not* let your washer move on to the spin cycle—you may have to restart the wash cycle to make sure you have enough time. Continue the felting process until no stitch definition can be seen, or you are satisfied with the look of the felted fabric.

Gently squeeze excess water from the felted item, then blot it with a bath towel to remove as much water as possible. Pull the felted item into the desired shape and let air dry. In humid climates, a fan may be needed to accelerate the drying process.

Skirt
the Issue

Crocheted skirts can be a challenge—until now, of course! This skirt by designer Andee Graves is perfect. She addresses all the points on any wish list: The lightweight wool-blend yarn holds its shape without adding weight, the tight stitch pattern only opens up at the bottom edge (where we can show a little skin without fear of flashing), and the wrap waist adjusts to fit comfortably. It's a flirty addition to any wardrobe. **DESIGNED BY ANDEE GRAVES**

Tip: The button closure at the wrap waistband allows for adjustability in fit. I added several buttons to my skirt so I could wear a range of blouses with it. I just tighten the waistband when I want a higher-waisted skirt for tucking in my shirts and loosen it for a low-slung look.

SKILL LEVEL
Intermediate

FINISHED SIZE
Waist: L, XL, 2X, 3X, 4X, 5X; 34 (38, 42, 46½, 51, 55) in.
Length: 24 in.

YARN
Premier Yarns Serenity Sock Weight; 9 (9, 10, 10, 11, 13) skeins Charcoal, #DN150-11 (1.76 oz/230 yds); 1,853 (2,056, 2,259, 2,508, 2,733, 2,959) yds fingering weight yarn (CYCA 1, Super Fine, see p. 146)

NOTIONS
Hook size D/3 U.S. (3.25 mm) and E/4 U.S. (3.5 mm) *or size needed to obtain gauge*
Stitch markers
Tapestry needle
2 decorative buttons, ⅝ in. in diameter
1 plain button, ⅝ in. in diameter
Sewing needle and thread

GAUGE
24 sts and 24 rows = 4 in. in patt st

NOTES
Skirt is worked from the waist foundation down.
To increase the length of the upper part of the skirt, repeat Rows 43–48 as many times as needed. To increase the length of the lower skirt, repeat Rows 66–69 as many times as needed.

SPECIAL STITCHES
Small Shell (sm Sh): (2 dc, ch 2, sc) in indicated st/sp.
Shell (Sh): (2 tr, ch 2, dc) in indicated st/sp.
Small V-Stitch (sm V-st): (dc, ch 2, sc) in indicated st/sp.
V-Stitch (V-st): (tr, ch 2, dc) in indicated st/sp.

Skirt

Using hook size D/3 (U.S. (3.25 mm), ch 307 (343, 379, 419, 459, 495).
Row 1 Sc in back bump of 2nd ch from hook and in back bump of each ch to end, place marker in 42nd st from each end of row (move these markers up each row as worked; if there is an inc in the marked st, move marker to 1st st of inc). Ch 1, turn. 306 (342, 378, 418, 458, 494) sc.

continued on page 132

Row 2 Sk 1st st, *sc in next st, dc next st*, rep from * to * across to 1st marker, sc and dc in marked st (inc made), **continue repeating from * to * for next 14 sts, then inc in next st; rep from ** to last marker, then rep from * to * to 2nd st from the end of row, sl st in last st of row. Ch 1, turn. 319 (358, 396, 439, 481, 520) sts.

Row 3 Sk 1st st, dc in each sc, and sc in each dc of previous row across to 2nd st from the end of row, sl st in last st of row. Ch 1, turn.

Row 4 Sk 1st st, sc in each st across to 2nd st from the end of row. Ch 1, turn.

Row 5 Sk 1st st, *sc in next st, dc next st*, rep from * to * to 2nd st from end of row, sl st in last st. Ch 1, turn.

Row 6 Rep Row 3.

Rows 7 and 13 Rep Row 4.

Rows 8 and 14 Rep Row 2.

Rows 9 and 15 Rep Row 3.

Rows 10 and 16 Rep Row 4.

Rows 11 and 17 Rep Row 5.

Rows 12 and 18 Rep Row 3.

HIGH HIP

Rows 19, 25, 31, and 37 Rep Row 4.

Rows 20, 26, 32, and 38 Sk 1st st, *sc in next st, dc in next st*, rep from * to * across to 1st marker, inc in marked st, **continue repeating from * to * for next 64 sts, inc in next st; rep from ** across to last marker, then rep from * to * across to 2nd st from end of row, sl st in last st of row. Ch 1, turn.

Rows 21, 27, 33, and 39 Rep Row 3.

Rows 22, 28, 34, and 40 Rep Row 4.

Rows 23, 29, 35, and 41 Rep Row 5.

Rows 24, 30, 36, and 42 Rep Row 3. Place marker in 1st and last sts of Row 42, which marks the end of the tapered decreases. Change to the larger hook.

Rows 43, 49, and 55 Sc in each st to end of row. Ch 1, turn.

Rows 44, 50, and 56 {*Sc in next st, dc next st*, rep from * to * for next 64 sts, then sc and dc in next st} rep {} to last st of row. Ch 1, turn.

Rows 45, 51, and 57 Dc in scs and sc in dcs of previous row, work to end of row. Ch 1, turn.

Rows 46, 52, and 58 Sc in each st to end of row. Ch 1, turn.

Rows 47, 53, and 59 *Sc in next st, dc in next st*, rep from * to * to end of row. Ch 1, turn.

Rows 48, 54, and 60 Sc in dcs, dc in scs to end of row. Ch 1, turn.

Row 61 Sc in each st to end of row. Ch 2, turn.

Sizes L (XL, 2X, 3X, 5X) only:

Row 62 Ch 2, turn, *(sk 2 sts, sm Sh in next st) 12 times, (sk 1 st, sm Sh in next st) 2 times*, rep from * to * until 3 sts from end of row, sk 2 sts, hdc in last st of row.

Size 4X only:

Row 62 Ch 2, turn, *(sk 2 sts, sm Sh in next st) 12 times, (sk 1 st, sm Sh in next st) 2 times*, rep from * to * until 4 sts from end of row, sk 1 st, sm Sh in next st, sk 1 st, hdc in last st of row.

For all sizes:

Row 63 Sm Sh in each ch-2 sp of previous row, hdc 2nd ch of beg ch-2. Ch 2, turn. 86 (101, 115, 130, 147, 159) sm Sh.

Rows 64 and 65 Rep Row 63.

Row 66 *Sm Sh in next 12 ch-2 sps, sm V-st between last sm Sh and next sm Sh*, rep from * to * until end of row, hdc in 2nd ch of beg ch-2. Ch 2, turn. 93 (109, 124, 140, 159, 172) sm Sh.

Row 67 Sm Sh in each ch-2 sp of previous row, hdc 2nd ch of beg ch-2. Ch 2, turn.

Rows 68 and 69 Rep Row 67.

Rep Rows 66–69 to increase length of lower skirt as desired.

Row 70 Rep Row 66. 100 (118, 134, 151, 172, 186) sm Sh.

Rows 71, 72, and 73 Rep Row 67. End last rep with Ch 3, turn.

Row 74 *Sh in next ch-2 sp, sm Sh next ch-2 sp* rep from * to * to end of row, dc in 2nd ch of beg ch-2. Ch 3, turn.

Row 75 *Sm Sh in ch-2 sps of Shs, Sh in ch-2 sps of sm Shs * rep from * to * to end of row, dc in 3rd ch of beg ch-3. Ch 3, turn.

Rows 76 and 77 Rep Row 75.

Rows 78, 79, 80, and 81 Sh in each ch-2 sp of previous row, dc in 3rd ch of beg ch-3. Ch 3, turn.

Row 82 *Sh in next 18 ch-2 sps, V-st between last Sh and next Sh*, rep from * to * until end of row, dc in 3rd ch of beg ch-3. Ch 3, turn.

Row 83 Rep Row 78. 105 (124, 141, 159, 181, 196) sm Sh.

Rows 84 and 85 Rep Row 78. End off (after blocking, the skirt will be 24 in. long).

Waistband

Row 1 With WS facing, attach yarn at right-hand end of starting ch, using hook size D/3 U.S. (3.25 mm), ch 1, sc in each st along row.

Row 2 Ch 4, turn, tr in each st to end of row.

Row 3 Ch 1, turn, sc in each st to end of row. End off.

EDGING (REINFORCE WAISTBAND)

With RS facing, attach yarn at the base of Row 42 on the right-hand end, sc evenly along sides of rows up to waistband.

Sc in the end of waistband Row 1, 3 sc in end of Row 2 (around tr sts), sc in end of Row 3, ch 1, sl st in each st along top of waistband to opposite end, ch 1, sc in end of waistband Row 3, 3 sc in end of Row 2, sc in end of Row 1.

Sl st/surface ch at base of each tr st of waistband Row 2, return with sl st/surface ch in base of each sc of Row 1, sl st into last sc of edging on end of waistband.

Sc evenly along sides of dec rows to Row 42. End off.

Finish

Weave in all ends and block gently to length. Using the sewing needle and thread, sew the 2 decorative buttons to the RS of the waistband ends and sew the plain flat button to the WS of outside waistband end.

Skirt the Issue Schematic

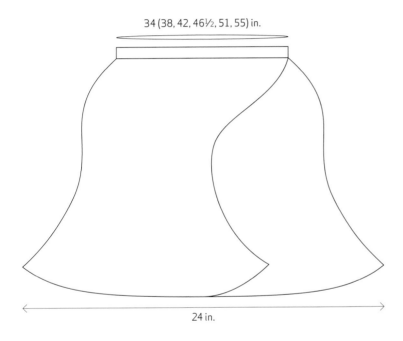

34 (38, 42, 46½, 51, 55) in.

24 in.

Aureate Vest

A little bit of beading dresses up a simple cotton vest. The Aureate Vest is cropped in the back so the vertical details on the front can hang true without pulling out of shape. Triple-check your back neck-to-waist measurement and compare it to the schematic, making any adjustments needed, for a perfect fit.

DESIGNED BY LINDSEY STEPHENS

Tip: The beads used here match the yarn they were strung on for a subtle sparkle. To up the glitz quotient, use brighter beads with more contrast—maybe gold, silver, or crystal with an aurora borealis finish.

SKILL LEVEL
Intermediate

FINISHED BUST
L (XL, 2X, 3X 4X, 5X); 45½ (52, 54½, 60, 63½, 66½) in.

YARN
Patons® Grace; 6 (6, 6, 7, 8, 9) skeins Taupe, #62012 (MC) and 1 (1, 1, 1, 2, 2) skein(s) Wildberry, #62436 (CC) (1.75 oz/136 yds); 660 (730, 770, 855, 930, 975) yds MC and 135 (135, 135, 135, 160, 160) yds CC sport weight yarn (CYCA 3, Light, see p. 146)

NOTIONS
Hook size F/5 U.S. (3.75 mm) *or size needed to obtain gauge*
279 (288, 288, 294, 309, 309) triangle beads, size 5/0
Stitch marker
Tapestry needle
Big eye beading needle, or hand sewing needle with any color of thread

GAUGE
10 V-st = 6¼ in.; 10 rows = 3 in.

NOTES
Vest is worked from the bottom up.
For color changes, work the last (yo, pull through loop) of each st in the color of the next st being made.
Directions indicate number of beads to pre-string for entire section of garment.

SPECIAL STITCHES
Beaded single crochet (bsc) = insert hook in stitch, yo, pull up a lp, push bead up to st, yo, pull through 2 lps on hook.
V stitch (V-st) = (dc, ch1, dc) in indicated st.

Back

With MC, ch 126 (141, 147, 159, 168, 174).
Row 1 (WS) Sc in 2nd ch from the hook and in each ch across. Ch 3 (counts as dc here and throughout), turn. 125 (140, 146, 158, 167, 173) sc.
Row 2 *Sk 1 sc, (dc, ch1, dc) in next sc, sk 1 sc; rep from * across, ending with dc in last sc. Ch 1, turn. 41 (46, 48, 52, 55, 57) V-st.
Row 3 Sc in each dc and ch-1 sp across. Ch 3, turn. 121 (140, 146, 158, 167, 173) sc.
Row 4 Rep Row 2.
Row 5 Sc in 1st dc, sc2tog in next dc and ch-1 sp, sc2tog in next 2 dc, sc2tog in next ch-1 sp and dc, sc in each dc and ch-1 sp across ending with (sc2tog in next dc and ch-1 sp, sc2tog in next 2 dc, sc2tog in next ch-1 sp and dc) across last 2 V-sts, sc in last dc. Ch 3, turn. 115 (134, 140, 152, 161, 167) sc.
Row 6 Rep Row 2. 39 (44, 46, 50, 53, 55) V-st.
Row 7 Sc in each dc and ch-1 sp across. Ch 3, turn.
Row 8 Rep Row 2.

continued on page 136

Rows 9–12 (12, 12, 12, 12, 10) Rep Rows 7–8 2 (2, 2, 2, 2, 1) more time(s).

Rep Rows 5–12 (12, 12, 12, 12, 10) twice more. 35 (40, 42, 46, 49, 51) V-st.

BUST

Row 1 Sc in each dc and ch-1 sp across. Ch 3, turn.
Row 2 *Sk 1 sc, V-st in next sc, sk 1 sc; rep from * across, ending with dc in last sc. Ch 1, turn.
Row 3 Sc in each dc and ch-1 sp across, turn.
Rep Rows 2–3 3 (1, 1, 0, 0, 2) more times, end off.

ARMHOLE SHAPING

Row 1 With RS facing, join yarn in 10th (10th, 10th, 10th, 13th, 13th) sc, ch 3, *sk 1 sc, V-st in next sc, sk 1 sc; rep from * 28 (33, 35, 39, 40, 42) times, dc in next sc. Ch 1, turn, leaving remaining sc unworked. 29 (34, 36, 40, 41, 43) V-st.
Row 2 Sc in 1st dc, sc2tog in next dc and ch-1sp, sc2tog in next 2 dc, sc2tog in next ch-1 sp and dc, sc in each dc and ch-1 sp across, ending with (sc2tog in next dc and ch-1 sp, sc2tog in next 2 dc, sc2tog in next ch-1 sp and dc) across last 2 V-sts, sc in last dc. Ch 3, turn. 83 (98, 104, 116, 119, 125) sc.
Row 3 *Sk 1 sc, V-st in next sc, sk 1 sc; rep from * across, ending with dc in last sc. Ch 1, turn. 27 (32, 34, 38, 39, 41) V-st.
Rep Rows 2–3 1 (3, 3, 4, 4, 4) more time(s). 25 (26, 28, 30, 31, 33) V-st.
Row 6 (10, 10, 12, 12, 12) Sc in each dc and ch-1 sp across. Ch 3, turn.
Row 7 (11, 11, 13, 13, 13) *Sk 1 sc, V-st in next sc, sk 1 sc; rep from * across, ending with dc in last sc. Ch 1, turn.
Rep Rows 6–7 (10–11, 10–11, 12–13, 12–13, 12–13) 6 (6, 6, 6, 7, 8) more times.
String 45 (48, 48, 48, 51, 51) beads onto CC.
Row 20 (24, 24, 26, 28, 30) With MC, ch 1, sc in each of next dc and ch-1 sps until a total of 16 (16, 19, 22, 22, 25) sc have been worked, with CC (sc in dc, bsc in ch-1 sp, sc in dc) 15 (16, 16, 16, 17, 17) times, join another ball of MC, sc in each dc and ch-1 sp across, turn.
Row 21 (25, 25, 27, 29, 31) With MC, ch 3, **sk 1 sc, V-st in next sc, sk 1 sc; rep from ** 4 (4, 5, 6, 6, 7) times, with CC *sk 1 sc, V-st in next sc, sk 1 sc; rep from * 14 (15, 15, 15, 16, 16) times, with MC (sk 1 sc, V-st in next sc, sk 1 sc) across, dc in last sc, turn.
Rep Rows 20–21 (24–25, 24–25, 26–27, 28–29, 30–31) once more.
Rep Row 20 (24, 24, 26, 28, 30), place marker in 26th (26th, 29th, 32nd, 32nd, 35th) sc.

RIGHT SHOULDER SHAPING

Row 1 With MC, ch 3, **sk 1 sc, V-st in next sc, sk 1 sc; rep from ** 4 (4, 5, 6, 6, 7) times, with CC *sk 1 sc, V-st in next sc, sk 1 sc; rep from * 2 times, dc in next sc, turn, leaving remaining sts unworked. 8 (8, 9, 10, 10, 11) V-st.
Row 2 With CC, ch 4 (counts as tr), tr in next dc, tr in next ch-1 sp, tr in next dc, dc in next dc, dc in next ch-1 sp, dc in next dc, hdc in next dc, hdc in next ch-1 sp, hdc in next dc, with MC sc in each dc and ch-1 sp across, end off.

LEFT SHOULDER SHAPING

Row 1 With RS facing, join CC yarn in marked sc, ch 3, *sk 1 sc, V-st in next sc, sk 1 sc; rep from * 2 times, with MC (sk 1 sc, V-st in next sc, sk 1 sc) across, dc in last sc, turn. 8 (8, 9, 10, 10, 11) V-st.
Row 2 With MC, sc in dc, (sc in next dc, sc in ch-1 sp, sc in next dc) 5 (5, 6, 7, 7, 8) times, with CC, hdc in next dc, hdc in next ch-1 sp, hdc in next dc, dc in next dc, dc in next ch-1 sp, dc in next dc, tr in next dc, tr in next ch-1 sp, tr in each of next 2 dc, end off.

Right Front

String 117 (120, 120, 123, 129, 129) beads onto CC. With CC, ch 2.
Row 1 (WS) Bsc in 2nd ch from the hook, turn. 1 sc.
Row 2 Ch 3 (counts as dc), (dc, ch 2, dc) all in bsc, turn. 3 dc.
Row 3 Ch 1, bsc in dc, 2 sc in ch-2 sp, bsc in next dc, sc in last dc, turn. 5 sc.
Row 4 Ch 3, V-st in next bsc, (V-st, ch 3, dtr) in next bsc, turn. 2 V-st.
Row 5 With MC, ch 1, sc in dtr, with CC (sc, bsc, sc) in ch-3 sp, (sc in next dc, bsc in ch-1 sp, sc in next dc) 2 times, sc in last dc, turn. 11 sc.
Row 6 With CC, ch 3, V-st in each of next 3 bsc, with MC (V-st, ch 3, dtr) in last sc, turn. 4 V-st.
Row 7 With MC, ch 1, sc in dtr, 3 sc in ch-3 sp, sc in next dc, sc in ch-1 sp, sc in next dc, with CC (sc in next dc, bsc in ch-1 sp, sc in next dc) 3 times, sc in last dc, turn. 17 sc.
Row 8 With CC, ch 3, V-st in each of next 3 bsc, sk next sc, with MC (sk next sc, V-st in next sc, sk next sc) across, working (V-st, ch 3, dtr) in last sc, turn. 6 V-st.
Row 9 With MC, ch 1, sc in dtr, 3 sc in ch-3 sp, (sc in next dc, sc in ch-1 sp, sc in next dc) across, working (with CC, *sc in next dc, bsc in ch-1 sp, sc in next dc; rep from * 2 times) across last 3 V-sts, sc in last dc, turn.

Row 10 With CC, ch 3, V-st in each of next 3 bsc, sk next sc, with MC (sk next sc, V-st in next sc, sk next sc) across, working (V-st, ch 3, dtr) in last sc, turn. 8 V-st. Rep Rows 9–10 for 3 (4, 5, 6, 6, 7) more times. 14 (16, 18, 20, 20, 22) V-st.

WAIST SHAPING

Row 1 With MC, ch 1, sc in dtr, 3 sc in ch-3 sp, (sc in next dc, sc in ch-1 sp, sc in next dc) across, working (with CC, *sc in next dc, bsc in ch-1 sp, sc in next dc; rep from * 2 times) across last 3 V-sts, sc in last dc, turn. 47 (53, 59, 65, 65, 71) sc.

Sizes L (XL, 4X) only:
Row 2 With CC, ch 3, V-st in each of next 3 bsc, sk next sc, with MC *sk next sc, V-st in next sc, sk next sc; rep from * across, dc in last sc, turn. 15 (17, 21) V-st.
Row 3 With MC, ch 1, sc in 1st dc, 2 sc in next dc, 2 sc in next ch-1 sp, 2 sc in next dc, (sc in next dc, sc in ch-1 sp, sc in next dc) across, working (with CC, *sc in next dc, bsc in ch-1 sp, sc in next dc; rep from * 2 times) across last 3 V-sts, sc in last dc, turn. 50 (56, 68) sc.

All sizes:
Row 4 (4, 2, 2, 4, 2) With CC, ch 3, V-st in each of next 3 bsc, sk next sc, with MC *sk next sc, V-st in next sc, sk next sc; rep from * across, dc in last sc, turn. 16 (18, 19, 21, 22, 23) V-st.
Row 5 (5, 3, 3, 5, 3) With MC, ch 1, (sc in next dc, sc in ch-1 sp, sc in next dc) across, working (with CC, *sc in next dc, bsc in ch-1 sp, sc in next dc; rep from * 2 times) across last 3 V-sts, sc in last dc, turn.
Rep Row 4 (4, 2, 2, 4, 2) once.

DECREASE SHAPING

Row 1 With MC, ch 1, sc in 1st dc, sc2tog in next dc and ch-1 sp, sc2tog in next 2 dc, sc2tog in next ch-1 sp and dc, sc in each dc and ch-1 sp across, working (with CC, *sc in next dc, bsc in ch-1 sp, sc in next dc; rep from * 2 times) across last 3 V-sts, sc in last dc, turn. 47 (53, 56, 62, 65, 68) sc.
Row 2 With CC, ch 3, V-st in each of next 3 bsc, sk next sc, with MC *sk next sc, V-st in next sc, sk next sc; rep from * across, dc in last sc, turn. 15 (17, 18, 20, 21, 22) V-st.
Row 3 With MC, ch 1, (sc in next dc, sc in ch-1 sp, sc in next dc) across, working (with CC, *sc in next dc, bsc in ch-1 sp, sc in next dc; rep from * 2 times) across last 3 V-sts, sc in last dc, turn.
Row 4 Rep Row 2.

Rows 5–8 (8, 8, 8, 8, 6) Rep Rows 3–4 2 (2, 2, 2, 2, 1) more time(s).
Rep Rows 1–8 (8, 8, 8, 8, 6) twice more. 13 (15, 16, 18, 19, 20) V-st.

BUST

Row 1 With MC, ch 1, (sc in next dc, sc in ch-1 sp, sc in next dc) across, working (with CC, *sc in next dc, bsc in ch-1 sp, sc in next dc; rep from * 2 times) across last 3 V-sts, sc in last dc, turn.
Row 2 With CC, ch 3, V-st in each of next 3 bsc, sk next sc, with MC *sk next sc, V-st in next sc, sk next sc; rep from * across, dc in last sc, turn.
Row 3 Rep Row 1.
Rep Rows 2–3 3 (1, 1, 0, 0, 2) more times, do not end off.

ARMHOLE SHAPING

Row 1 With CC, ch 3, V-st in each of next 3 bsc, sk next sc, with MC *sk next sc, V-st in next sc, sk next sc; rep from * 6 (8, 9, 11, 11, 12) times, dc in next sc, turn leaving remaining sts unworked. 10 (12, 13, 15, 15, 16) V-st.
Row 2 With MC, ch 1, sc in 1st dc, sc2tog in next dc and ch-1 sp, sc2tog in next 2 dc, sc2tog in next ch-1 sp and dc, sc in each dc and ch-1 sp across, working (with CC, *sc in next dc, bsc in ch-1 sp, sc in next dc; rep from * 2 times) across last 3 V-sts, sc in last dc, turn. 29 (35, 38, 44, 44, 47) sc.
Row 3 With CC, ch 3, V-st in each of next 3 bsc, sk next sc, with MC *sk next sc, V-st in next sc, sk next sc; rep from * across, dc in last sc, turn. 9 (11, 12, 14, 14, 15) V-st.
Rep Rows 2–3 for 1 (3, 3, 4, 4, 4) more time(s). 8 (8, 9, 10, 10, 11) V-st.

SHOULDER

Row 1 With MC, ch 1, (sc in next dc, sc in ch-1 sp, sc in next dc) across, working (with CC, *sc in next dc, bsc in ch-1 sp, sc in next dc; rep from * 2 times) across last 3 V-sts, sc in last dc, turn.
Row 2 With CC, ch 3, V-st in each of next 3 bsc, sk next sc, with MC *sk next sc, V-st in next sc, sk next sc; rep from * across, dc in last sc, turn.
Rep Rows 1–2 9 (9, 9, 9, 10, 11) more times.

SHOULDER SHAPING

Row 1 With MC, sc in dc, (sc in next dc, sc in ch-1 sp, sc in next dc) 5 (5, 6, 7, 7, 8) times, with CC, hdc in next dc, hdc in next ch-1 sp, hdc in next dc, dc in next dc, dc in

continued on page 138

next ch-1 sp, dc in next dc, tr in next dc, tr in next ch-1 sp, tr in each of next 2 dc, end off.

Left Front

String 117 (120, 120, 123, 129, 129) beads onto CC. With CC, ch 2.

Row 1 (WS) Bsc in 2nd ch from the hook, turn. 1 sc.

Row 2 Ch 5 (counts as dc plus ch 2), 2 dc in bsc, turn. 3 dc.

Row 3 Ch 1, sc in 1st dc, bsc in next dc, 2 sc in ch-2 sp, bsc in last dc, turn. 5 sc.

Row 4 Ch 8 (counts as dtr plus ch 3), V-st in each bsc, dc in last sc, turn. 2 V-st.

Row 5 Ch 1, sc in 1st dc, (sc in dc, bsc in ch-1 sp, sc in dc) twice, (sc, bsc, sc) in ch-3 sp, with MC, sc in dtr, turn. 11 sc.

Row 6 With MC, ch 8, V-st in 1st sc, with CC, V-st in each bsc, dc in last sc, turn. 4 V-st.

Row 7 With CC, ch 1, sc in 1st dc (sc in dc, bsc in ch-1 sp, sc in dc) 3 times, with MC, sc in dc, sc in ch-1 sp, sc in dc, 3 sc in ch-3 sp, sc in dtr, turn. 17 sc.

Row 8 With MC, ch 8, V-st in 1st sc, *sk 1 sc, V-st in next sc, sk 1 sc; rep from * once, with CC, V-st in each bsc, dc in last sc, turn. 6 V-st.

Row 9 With CC, ch 1, sc in 1st dc, (sc in dc, bsc in ch-1 sp, sc in dc) 3 times, with MC, sc in each dc and ch-1 sp across ending with 3 sc in ch-3 sp, sc in dtr, turn. 23 sc.

Row 10 With MC, ch 8, (dc, ch-1 dc) in 1st sc, *sk 1 sc, V-st in next sc, sk 1 sc; rep from * across, ending with (with CC, V-st in each bsc, dc in last sc) across last 10 sts, turn. 8 (dc, ch-1 dc).

Rep Rows 9–10 for 3 (4, 5, 6, 6, 7) more times. 14 (16, 18, 20, 20, 22) V-st.

WAIST SHAPING

Row 1 With CC, sc in 1st dc, (sc in dc, bsc in ch-1 sp, sc in dc) 3 times, with MC, sc in each dc and ch-1 sp across ending with 3 sc in ch-3 sp, sc in dtr, turn. 47 (53, 59, 65, 65, 71) sc.

Sizes L (XL, 4X) only:

Row 2 With MC, ch 3, *sk 1 sc, V-st in next sc, sk 1 sc; rep from * across ending with (with CC, V-st in each bsc, dc in last sc) across last 10 sts, turn. 15 (17, 21) V-st.

Row 3 With CC, sc in 1st dc, (sc in dc, bsc in ch-1 sp, sc in dc) 3 times, with MC, sc in each dc and ch-1 sp across ending with (2 sc in dc, 2 sc in ch-1 sp, 2 sc in dc, sc in last dc), turn. 50 (56, 68) sc.

All sizes:

Row 4 (4, 2, 2, 4, 2) With MC, ch 3, *sk 1 sc, V-st in next sc, sk 1 sc; rep from * across ending with (with CC, V-st in each bsc, dc in last sc) across last 10 sts, turn. 16 (18, 19, 21, 22, 23) V-st.

Row 5 (5, 3, 3, 5, 3) With CC, sc in 1st dc, (sc in dc, bsc in ch-1 sp, sc in dc) 3 times, with MC, sc in each dc and ch-1 sp across, turn.

Rep Row 4 (4, 2, 2, 4, 2) once.

DECREASE SHAPING

Row 1 With CC ch 1, sc in 1st dc, (sc in dc, bsc in ch-1 sp, sc in dc) 3 times, with MC sc in each dc and ch-1 sp across ending with (sc2tog in next dc and ch-1 sp, sc2tog in next 2 dc, sc2tog in next ch-1sp and dc) across last 2 V-sts, sc in last dc, turn. 47 (53, 56, 62, 65, 68) sc.

Row 2 With MC, ch 3, *sk 1 sc, V-st in next sc, sk 1 sc; rep from * across ending with (with CC, V-st in each bsc, dc in last sc) across last 10 sts, turn. 15 (17, 18, 20, 21, 22) V-st.

Row 3 With CC, sc in 1st dc, (sc in dc, bsc in ch-1 sp, sc in dc) 3 times, with MC, sc in each dc and ch-1 sp across, turn.

Row 4 Rep Row 2.

Rows 5–8 (8, 8, 8, 8, 6) Rep Rows 3–4 2 (2, 2, 2, 2, 1) more time(s).

Rep Rows 1–8 (8, 8, 8, 8, 6) twice. 13 (15, 16, 18, 19, 20) V-st.

BUST

Row 1 With CC, sc in 1st dc, (sc in dc, bsc in ch-1 sp, sc in dc) 3 times, with MC, sc in each dc and ch-1 sp across, turn.

Row 2 With MC, ch 3, *sk 1 sc, V-st in next sc, sk 1 sc; rep from * across ending with (with CC, V-st in each bsc, dc in last sc) across last 10 sts, turn.

Row 3 Rep Row 1.

Rep Rows 2–3 for 3 (1, 1, 0, 0, 2) more time(s), end off.

ARMHOLE SHAPING

Row 1 With RS facing, join MC in 10th (10th, 10th, 10th, 13th, 13th) sc, ch 3, *sk 1 sc, V-st in next sc, sk 1 sc; rep from *6 (8, 9, 11, 11, 12) times, with CC, V-st in each of next 3 bsc, dc in last sc, turn. 10 (12, 13, 15, 15, 16) V-st.

Row 2 With CC, ch 1, sc in 1st dc, (sc in dc, bsc in ch-1 sp, sc in dc) 3 times, with MC, sc in each dc and ch-1 sp across, ending with (sc2tog in next dc and ch-1 sp, sc2tog in next 2 dc, sc2tog in next ch-1 sp and dc) across last 2 V-sts, sc in last dc, turn.

Row 3 With MC, ch 3, *sk 1 sc, V-st in next sc, sk 1 sc; rep from * across ending with (with CC, V-st in each bsc, dc in last sc) across last 10 sts, turn. 9 (11, 12, 14, 14, 15) V-st. Rep Rows 2–3 1 (3, 3, 4, 4, 4) more time(s). 8 (8, 9, 10, 10, 11) V-st.

SHOULDER

Row 1 With CC, sc in 1st dc, (sc in dc, bsc in ch-1 sp, sc in dc) 3 times, with MC sc in each dc and ch-1 sp across, turn.

Row 2 With MC, ch 3, *sk 1 sc, V-st in next sc, sk 1 sc; rep from * across ending with (with CC, V-st in each bsc, dc in last sc) across last 10 sts, turn.

Rep Rows 1–2 9 (9, 9, 9, 10, 11) more times.

SHOULDER SHAPING

Row 1 With CC, ch 4, tr in next dc, tr in next ch-1 sp, tr in next dc, dc in next dc, dc in next ch-1 sp, dc in next dc, hdc in next dc, hdc in next ch-1 sp, hdc in next dc, with MC sc in each dc and ch-1 sp across, end off.

Finishing

Weave in ends. Block to finished measurements. Seam pieces together along sides and shoulders.

Aureate Vest Schematics

BACK

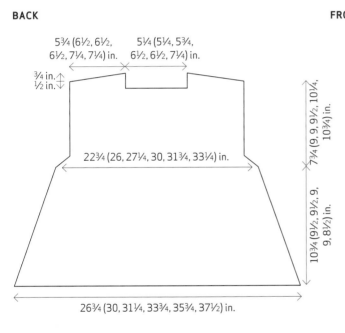

FRONT

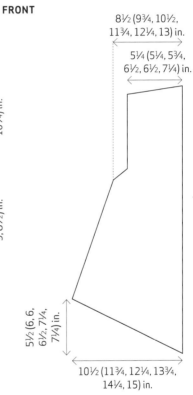

Aureate Vest Stitch Diagram

Techniques and Stitches

Project planning isn't just about the stitching—what elevates a simple sweater from will-do-in-a-pinch to "wow" is the details.

You may not have run across all of these special techniques before, so welcome to the back of the book, where you can get a little extra how-to information. Don't be afraid to try something new! You may very well discover your favorite go-to technique here.

Reading Patterns

Here are just a few tips on reading patterns.

- Read all the way through the pattern before you start crocheting. Sometimes an instruction won't make sense until you have the work in process in your hands, but it's great to make note of shapings that take place at the same time. Make sure you know if you need to take neckline shaping into account while you are breezing through your armhole shaping, or you may wind up ripping out stitches.

- All of the patterns in this book are written in sizes L to 5X. If you see a series of numbers in parenthesis, for example, "Rep from * 5 (6, 6, 7, 7, 8) times," you need to use the number that refers to the size you are making. If there is a repeat number without parentheses, that number applies to all sizes.

- If you are starting a row or round of edging, the instructions may tell you to start here or there with a sc, a dc, or whatever stitch you need. In the olden days, you may have been instructed to join the yarn with a sl st and ch a set number needed for the first stitch, but I find a "standing start" looks much neater: Place a sl st on your hook, then work your first stitch as you normally would.

Linked Double Crochet (LDC)

Almost any stitch can be turned into a linked stitch, and linked stitches give a smoother, less textured appearance to large areas of plain stitching.

For linked double crochet, which is used in the Comely Cardigan on p. 76, the mechanics are almost identical to a row of regular double crochet, with one exception—the first yo.

There is one loop on your hook from the previous st or t-ch. Insert the hook top to bottom through the horizontal bar of the st previous (2nd of 3 ch if the t-ch), yo, and draw through the bar. Now the rest of the st is the same as a regular dc: yo, insert hook through next st, yo, draw through st, yo, draw through 2 loops on hook, yo, draw through 2 loops on hook. Work in this manner all the way across the row.

Use the same technique for linked half double crochet stitches, but after you draw your yo through the stitch, yo and draw through all loops on the hook.

Pre-Stringing Beads

The fastest way to pre-string beads is to use a big eye beading needle, often found at craft or specialty bead shops. These needles split right down the middle and can accommodate any size of yarn and/or bead. If that is not available to you, try the following trick with a sewing needle and thread. Make sure the needle you choose can pass easily through the bead you have chosen.

Cut a length of regular sewing thread about 12–14 in. long. Put *both* cut ends of the thread through the eye of the sewing needle in the same direction. You will have two cut ends showing on one side of the needle and a loop showing on the other side.

Put at least 6 in. more of your yarn through the thread loop and tug gently on the loop until it is 2 in. or less away from the sewing needle.

Thread the desired number of beads, a few at a time, onto the sewing needle, then slide them down the sewing thread and onto the yarn. It might be a bit of a tight squeeze until the beads get past the doubled amount of yarn, but the bead should slide easily up and down one strand of yarn. If it sticks or tugs, you should try again with larger beads or finer yarn.

It is always better to string too many beads than too few! Extras will just hang out on the working yarn, to be eliminated when the project is finished.

Crab Stitch (Reverse Single Crochet)

This simple, common edging creates a tailored finish that looks like applied I-cord. The trick is to work in the opposite direction as you normally stitch—left to right for right-handed crocheters or right to left for left-handed crocheters—while keeping the hook head oriented in the direction you normally stitch.

When working crab stitch in the round, you get a neater join if you work your final crab stitch right on top of the sc with which you started the round.

Blocking

Blocking goes a long way toward ensuring your finished garment fits the way you expect it to, and it makes your stitching look much neater to boot. To block a garment or piece of a garment, get it damp or wet, pin it to the desired shape, and allow it to air dry. Many people like to pin their garments to an ironing board or a set of clean foam floor mats, available at hardware stores, but the guest room bed or a thick pile of bath towels works just as well.

If you are planning on blocking your finished item—and you should be—block the gauge swatch first. This way you can test for colorfastness, and see if the blocking process causes your swatch to grow in ways you did not expect. Whatever the swatch does during this process, the finished item will do, too, so this way you can plan ahead and avoid any unhappy surprises.

Animal fibers hold a block very well; plant fibers like cotton and bamboo do not. Acrylic yarns vary wildly in how they react to blocking, so treat your gauge swatch like you wish to treat your finished item to test things out.

Many people like to use a steam iron instead of the slower process of washing an item and pinning it out. Steam irons have their place, but be careful you don't smash the iron down on your beautiful stitching, losing all of your stitch definition. In addition, if you overheat acrylic yarns (technically called "killing" the acrylic), they will lose what little elasticity they had in the first place. Some stitchers like to kill acrylics on purpose, making a fabric that is shiny with lots of drape, but it isn't always the best use of the yarn.

Skill Level Key

BEGINNER: These projects use basic stitches and have minimal shaping.

EASY: These projects use repetitive stitch patterns, simple color changes, shaping, and finishing.

INTERMEDIATE: These projects use techniques such as basic lace or color patterns and have more advanced shaping and finishing.

Stitch Diagram Key

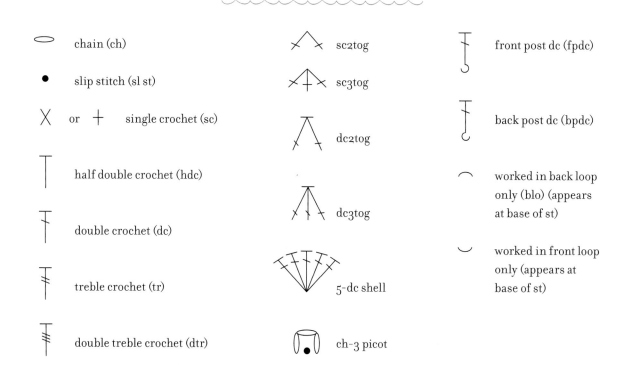

chain (ch)

slip stitch (sl st)

single crochet (sc)

half double crochet (hdc)

double crochet (dc)

treble crochet (tr)

double treble crochet (dtr)

sc2tog

sc3tog

dc2tog

dc3tog

5-dc shell

ch-3 picot

front post dc (fpdc)

back post dc (bpdc)

worked in back loop only (blo) (appears at base of st)

worked in front loop only (appears at base of st)

Sizing Chart

This is the sizing chart the guest designers and I used as a basis for the sizing in this book.

Of course, there is no one-size-fits-all pattern in the world, and each garment may have variations depending on how it is supposed to fit, and even the stitch multiple. Use this chart to decide what size in the pattern is most likely to fit you, and make your modifications from the actual measurements of your chosen garment.

	L	XL	2X	3X	4X	5X
Shirt Size	14–16	18–20	22–24	26–28	30–32	34–36
Bust	42½ in.	46½ in.	50½ in.	55 in.	59 in.	63 in.
Waist	34 in.	38 in.	42 in.	46½ in.	51 in.	55 in.
High Hip	43 in.	47 in.	51 in.	55 in.	59 in.	63 in.
Low Hip	45 in.	49 in.	53 in.	57 in.	61 in.	65 in.
Bicep	13¼ in.	14½ in.	15¾ in.	17 in.	18¼ in.	19½ in.
Center Back Neck to Waist	17½ in.	17½ in.	18 in.	18 in.	18½ in.	18½ in.
Shoulder to Shoulder Back	15½ in.	16½ in.	17½ in.	18½ in.	19½ in.	20½ in.
Armhole Depth	8 in.	8½ in.	9 in.	9½ in.	10 in.	10½ in.
Inside Arm Length	17½ in.	17½ in.	18 in.	18 in.	18½ in.	18½ in.

Hook Sizing and Abbreviations

Crochet Hook Sizes

MILLIMETER RANGE	U.S. SIZE RANGE
2.25 mm	B/1
2.75 mm	C/2
3.25 mm	D/3
3.5 mm	E/4
3.75 mm	F/5
4 mm	G/6
4.5 mm	7
5 mm	H/8
5.5 mm	I/9
6 mm	J/10
6.5 mm	K/10½
8 mm	L/11
9 mm	M/N-13
10 mm	N/P-15
15 mm	P/Q
16 mm	Q
19 mm	S

Crochet Abbreviations

Beg	Beginning	Patt	Pattern
Bet	Between	PM	Place marker
blo	Back Loop Only	Rep	Repeat
Bpdc	Back post double crochet	Rnd	Round
CC	Contrast color	RS	Right side
Ch	Chain	Sc	Single crochet
Cl	Cluster	Sc2tog	Single crochet 2 together
Dc	Double crochet	Sc3tog	Single crochet 3 together
Dc2tog	Double crochet 2 together, a decrease	Sk	Skip
Dc3tog	Double crochet 3 together, a double decrease	Sl st	Slip stitch
Dec	Decrease	Sp(s)	Space(s)
Endcl	End cluster	St	Stitch
Fpdc	Front post double crochet	Tbl	Through back loop only
G	Gram	T-ch	Turning chain
Hdc	Half double crochet	Tog	Together
Hdc2tog	Half double crochet 2 together, a decrease	Tr	Treble or triple crochet
Inc	Increase	WS	Wrong side
Ldc	Linked double crochet	Yd	Yard
Lhdc	Linked half double crochet	Yo	Yarn over
lp	loop		
MC	Main color		
Oz	Ounce		

Yarn Information

Berroco
Vintage DK (50% acrylic/
40% wool/10% nylon)
www.berroco.com

Brown Sheep Company
Lamb's Pride Bulky (85% wool/
15% mohair)
www.brownsheep.com

Caron International
Country (75% microdenier
acrylic/25% wool)
Spa (75% acrylic/25% bamboo)
www.caron.com;
www.naturallycaron.com

Cascade Yarns
Ultra Pima (100% pima cotton)
www.cascadeyarns.com

Crystal Palace Yarns
Mini Mochi (80% superwash
merino wool/20% nylon)
www.straw.com

Filatura Di Crosa
Nirvana (100% extrafine merino
wool)
Available from Tahki Stacy
Charles, Inc.
www.tahkistacycharles.com

Himalaya Yarn
Duke Silk (100% silk)
www.himalayayarn.com

Kollage Yarns
Riveting (95% recycled cotton/
5% other)
www.kollageyarns.com

Lion Brand Yarn Company
Amazing (53% wool/47% acrylic)
Wool-Ease (80% acrylic/20% wool)
www.lionbrand.com

Lorna's Laces Yarns
Shepherd Sport (100% superwash
merino wool)
www.lornaslaces.net

Patons Yarns
Grace (100% mercerized cotton)
www.patonsyarns.com

Plymouth Yarn Company Inc.
Zino (75% superwash wool/
25% nylon)
www.plymouthyarn.com

Premier Yarns
Alpaca Dance (75% acrylic/
25% alpaca)
Serenity Chunky Tweeds
(97% acrylic/3% viscose)
Serenity Sock Weight
(50% superwash wool/
25% bamboo/25% nylon)
www.premieryarns.com

Red Heart Yarn
LusterSheen (100% acrylic)
Sport (100% acrylic)
Super Saver (100% acrylic)
www.redheart.com

Rowan Yarn
Panama (55% viscose/
33% cotton/12% linen)
Distributed by Westminster Fibers
www.westminsterfibers.com
www.knitrowan.com

SWTC INC
Pure (100% SOYSILK®)
www.soysilk.com

Tilli Tomas
Disco Lights (90% spun silk/
10% petite sequins)
www.tillitomas.com

Buttons and Closures

Annie Adams Adornment
www.annieadams.com
Comely Cardigan, p. 76

Buttons, Etc.
www.buttonsetc.com
Banded Cowl, p. 106

Durango Button Company, Inc.
www.durangobutton.com
Peacoat for Rule Breakers, p. 90;
Essential Pullover, p. 20

Jul Designs
www.juldesigns.com
Traditional Cloak, p. 96

Standard Yarn Weights

YARN WEIGHT SYMBOL	YARN WEIGHT NAMES	TYPE OF YARNS IN CATEGORY	CROCHET GAUGE* *(ranges in single crochet to 4 inch)*	RECOMMENDED HOOK *(in Metric Size range)*	RECOMMENDED HOOK *(in U.S. Size range)*
CYCA **0**	Lace	Fingering 10-count crochet thread	32–42 double crochets**	Steel*** 1.6–1.4 mm	Steel*** 6, 7, 8 Regular hook B–1
CYCA **1**	Super Fine	Sock, Fingering, Baby	21–32 sts	2.25–3.5 mm	B–1 to E–4
CYCA **2**	Fine	Sport, Baby	16–20 sts	3.5–4.5 mm	E–4 to 7
CYCA **3**	Light	DK, Light Worsted	12–17 sts	4.5–5.5 mm	7 to I–9
CYCA **4**	Medium	Worsted, Afghan, Aran	11–14 sts	5.5–6.5 mm	I–9 to K–101/2
CYCA **5**	Bulky	Chunky, Craft, Rug	8–11 sts	6.5–9 mm	K–101/2 to M–13
CYCA **6**	Super Bulky	Bulky, Roving	5–9 sts	9 mm and larger	M–13 and larger

*   GUIDELINES ONLY: The above reflect the most commonly used gauges and needle or hook sizes for specific yarn categories.

**   Lace weight yarns are usually knitted or crocheted on larger needles and hooks to create lacy, openwork patterns. Accordingly, a gauge range is difficult to determine. Always follow the gauge stated in your pattern.

***   Steel crochet hooks are sized differently from regular hooks—the higher the number, the smaller the hook, which is the reverse of regular hook sizing.

Metric Equivalency Chart

One inch equals approximately 2.54 centimeters. To convert inches to centimeters, multiply the figure in inches by 2.54 and round off to the nearest half centimeter, or use the chart below, whose figures are rounded off (one centimeter equals 10 millimeters).

⅛ in. = 3 mm	4 in. = 10 cm	16 in. = 40.5 cm
¼ in. = 6 mm	5 in. = 12.5 cm	18 in. = 45.5 cm
³⁄₈ in. = 1 cm	6 in. = 15 cm	20 in. = 51 cm
½ in. = 1.3 cm	7 in. = 18 cm	21 in. = 53.5 cm
⅝ in. = 1.5 cm	8 in. = 20.5 cm	22 in. = 56 cm
¾ in. = 2 cm	9 in. = 23 cm	24 in. = 61 cm
⅞ in. = 2.2 cm	10 in. = 25.5 cm	25 in. = 63.5 cm
1 in. = 2.5 cm	12 in. = 30.5 cm	36 in. = 92 cm
2 in. = 5 cm	14 in. = 35.5 cm	45 in. = 114.5 cm
3 in. = 7.5 cm	15 in. = 38 cm	60 in. = 152 cm

Project Index

Essential Pullover, p. 20

Curvy Cowl-Neck Pullover, p. 24

Verdant Pullover, p. 28

Progressive Tunic, p. 35

Counterpoint Pullover, p. 40

Aperture Tunic, p. 46

Sweetheart Tank Top, p. 50

Perfect Base Tank Top, p. 54

Orange Marmalade Shell, p. 58

Essential Cardigan, p. 64

Dulcet Wrap Cardigan, p. 70

Comely Cardigan, p. 76

Simply Stripes Jacket, p. 81

Intertwined Poncho, p. 86

Peacoat for Rule Breakers, p. 90

Traditional Cloak, p. 96

Stratum Wrap, p. 102

Banded Cowl, p. 106

Coalesce Wrap, p. 110

Sensible Shawl, p. 114

Wrapt Top, p. 118

Shimmer Scarf, p. 124

Carryall, p. 127

Skirt the Issue, p. 130

Aureate Vest, p. 134

Index

About the Author

Mary Beth Temple is the author of several humor books for the knitting- and crochet-obsessed, as well as crochet booklets for home decor.

Her crochet and knitting patterns appear frequently in magazines, including *Interweave Crochet, Your Knitting Life,* and *Crochet Today,* and she is featured in many multiauthor books and yarn company publications. Mary Beth is also the owner and lead designer for the popular pattern line Hooked for Life, which is available online and in select independent yarn stores.

Last but certainly not least, Mary Beth Temple hosted the only all-crochet interactive podcast, Getting Loopy, a three-time winner of the Flamie Awards for Best Crochet Podcast, which boasts more than 200,000 downloads.

Visit Mary Beth online at www.hookedforlife publishing.com.

Guest Artists

Marly Bird is an avid crocheter and knitter who loves to share her passion with her students. Balancing her day as wife, mom, podcaster, designer, and teacher is a challenge, but Marly wouldn't change any of it! You can find more of her designs at www.thepurseworkshop .com and www.marlybird.com.

Andee Graves, owner of Two Hands Healing and Creative Arts, is a crochet designer, writer, artist, and teacher. She combines a lifelong passion for crocheting, sewing, and crafting with a strong interest in mathematics. Andee also teaches and writes about crochet techniques, designing, and healthy crafting practices for her blog and other online publications. She launched her independent pattern line M2H

Designs in fall 2010. Andee lives in the mountains of Colorado with her husband and two sons.

Lindsey Stephens is the crochet and knit designer behind www.poetryinyarn.com. She is a professional member of the Crochet Guild of America (CGOA) as well as a member of The National Needlearts Association (TNNA). Her designs have been published in a national magazine as well as by yarn companies. Lindsey teaches needle arts and crafting classes.

Charles Voth has been crocheting for 40 years. He started with doilies and potholders and soon lost interest; they didn't do much for his bedroom decor. At 15, he was designing knitwear for himself but never thought of using crochet to make a garment, as there were no examples of that in his native Colombia. After moving to Canada, he learned about fiber, drape, hand, and texture while working in a yarn store, and explored how his crochet designs could benefit from his understanding of yarn. Recently he has been exploring designing crochet for men and women's plus-sizes; www.charles vothdesigns.ca.

Karen Ratto Whooley learned to crochet from her Italian grandmother at age seven in 1974. In two hours she was literally "hooked." Never quite happy with the way a pattern was designed, she would always adjust something to suit her needs or create a pattern on her own. In 1998, Karen started designing and selling patterns. Since then, she has had patterns published by a variety of magazines and books. Karen is also a nationally recognized crochet instructor. A California native, Karen resides in the Seattle, Washington, area with her husband and two children. You can see her work and her upcoming classes and workshops at www.krwknit wear.com.